Devotions
for Kids

Presented to

_____

By

_____

On

_____

Devotions
for Kids

Edited by
Jill C. Lafferty

★

Illustrated by
Peter Grosshauser

SPARK
HOUSE
FAMILY
MINNEAPOLIS

First edition published 2016
Printed in China
22   21   20   19   18   17   16   1   2   3   4   5   6   7   8

Edited by Jill C. Lafferty
Cover design by Mighty Media
Cover illustration by Peter Grosshauser
Interior designed by Mighty Media and Tory Herman
Illustrations by Peter Grosshauser

Library of Congress Cataloging-in-Publication Data
Names: Lafferty, Jill C., editor. | Grosshauser, Peter, illustrator.
Title: Spark Story Bible devotions for kids / edited by Jill C. Lafferty ;
    illustrated by Peter Grosshauser.
Other titles: Bible devotions for kids | Devotions for kids
Description: Minneapolis : Sparkhouse Family, [2016] | Audience: Ages 5-8.- |
    Audience: K to grade 3.-
Identifiers: LCCN 2016006491 (print) | LCCN 2016012787 (ebook) | ISBN
    9781506417660 (alk. paper) | ISBN 9781506417776
Subjects: LCSH: Children--Prayers and devotions. | Bible stories,
    English--Juvenile literature.
Classification: LCC BS551.3 .S6342 2016 (print) | LCC BS551.3 (ebook) | DDC
    242.62--dc23
LC record available at http://lccn.loc.gov/2016006491

VN0003466; 9781506417660; AUG2016

Sparkhouse Family
510 Marquette Avenue
Minneapolis, MN 55402
sparkhouse.org

A Message for Grown-Ups

Cultivating a devotional life as a family is one way to grow closer to each other and closer to God. All parents long for meaningful moments with their children, but making that happen can be a challenge. That's why *Spark Story Bible Devotions for Kids* was created.

Each devotion includes a Bible story, discussion questions, a prayer, key verses, and an activity to do together as a family. Keep an eye out for Squiggles, the expressive caterpillar who will help spark children's engagement. As you explore 100 of the most beloved Bible stories, you will learn together how to apply the teachings and wisdom of the Scriptures to everyday life.

Spark Story Bible Devotions for Kids is illustrated by Peter Grosshauser, illustrator of the award-winning *Spark Story Bible*. These delightful images of biblical people, animals, and landscapes practically leap off the page as you explore God's Word together.

No matter when or where you read it, *Spark Story Bible Devotions for Kids* will bring the Bible to life and your family closer together. We hope these devotions become a cherished tradition in your family's life!

Blessings,

The Sparkhouse Family Team

Devotions from the Old Testament

Creation. 12

Adam and Eve 14

The First Sin 16

Noah's Ark. 18

Abram's Call 20

God's Promises to Abram. 22

Abraham and Sarah's Visitors 24

Rebekah and Isaac. .26

Isaac's Blessing 28

Joseph and His Brothers. 30

Pharaoh's Dreams 32

Joseph Helps His Family 34

Baby Moses. 36

The Burning Bush 38

Free from Slavery. 40

The Plagues. 42

The Red Sea 44

Manna, Quail, and Water. 46

The Ten Commandments. 48

The Battle of Jericho 50

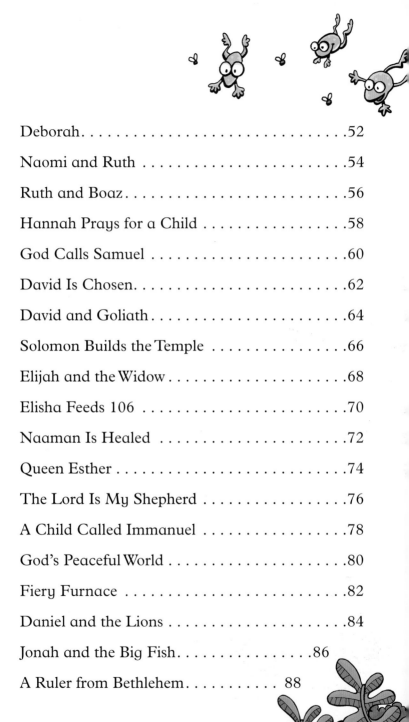

Deborah 52

Naomi and Ruth .54

Ruth and Boaz 56

Hannah Prays for a Child 58

God Calls Samuel .60

David Is Chosen 62

David and Goliath .64

Solomon Builds the Temple 66

Elijah and the Widow 68

Elisha Feeds 106 .70

Naaman Is Healed 72

Queen Esther 74

The Lord Is My Shepherd 76

A Child Called Immanuel 78

God's Peaceful World 80

Fiery Furnace 82

Daniel and the Lions 84

Jonah and the Big Fish 86

A Ruler from Bethlehem 88

Devotions from the New Testament

Angels Visit. 90

Mary Visits Elizabeth .92

Jesus Is Born. 94

Wise Men. 96

Simeon and Anna. 98

The Boy at the Temple 100

John the Baptist 102

Jesus' Baptism 104

Jesus Goes to Nazareth 106

Jesus Heals. 108

The Disciples 110

The Beatitudes 112

Love Your Enemies. 114

Do Not Worry 116

The Lord's Prayer 118

House on the Rock 120

A Storm 122

The Centurion's Servant 124

The Sower 126

Walking on Water 128

The Vineyard Workers 130

The Greatest Commandment 132

Jesus Blesses the Children 134

A Rich Man's Questions 136

Bartimaeus Sees .138

The Widow's Offering 140

Four Friends 142

Banquet with Simon 144

The Transfiguration 146

The Good Samaritan 148

Mary and Martha 150

The Lost Sheep and Lost Coin 152

The Prodigal Son. 154

Ten Men Healed 156

Zacchaeus 158

Wedding at Cana. 160

Woman at the Well .162

Jesus Feeds 5,006 164

The Good Shepherd. 166

Lazarus 168

Palm Sunday. 170

The Last Supper 172

Jesus Is Betrayed 174

The Day Jesus Died .176

The Empty Tomb. 178

The Road to Emmaus 180

Doubting Thomas 182

The Great Commission 184

The Ascension 186

The Holy Spirit 188

Early Believers 190

Peter Heals. 192

Saul to Paul 194

An Angel Frees Peter 196

Lydia 198

Paul and Silas 200

Paul's Letters 202

Many Members, One Body 204

Love Is 206

Fruit of the Spirit 208

Paul and the Philippians 210

Creation

In the beginning, God created. God made the land and sea. God spoke life over the earth and it bloomed with plants and flowers. "Let there be animals!" God said, and the earth was filled with creatures that wiggle, splash, gallop, and creep. God made human beings last. Finally, God looked over the entire creation and said it was very good. Then God rested.

What's your favorite part of creation? When have you created something?

Key Verse

God made the wild animals according to their kinds, the livestock according to their kinds, and all the creatures that move along the ground according to their kinds. And God saw that it was good.

Genesis 1:25

Thank you, creator God, for this earth full of life! Amen.

 Try this!

God created us, and we are creative too! Use chenille craft stems to make your own new creations. What new animals and plants can you create? What other ways do people create new things?

There's MORE to this story!

Read the WHOLE story in your Bible together!

You can find it in the first book in the Bible: Genesis 1:1—2:4

In the Spark Story Bible, look for "Creation" on page 6.

13

Adam and Eve

God created a beautiful world and asked Adam and Eve to help take care of it. Adam even got to name all the animals! Adam and Eve were amazed when they looked around at everything in God's wonderful world. They were happy to help care for God's creation, and God was happy for their help.

What is your favorite animal? How do you care for the world God created?

Key Verse

The LORD God took the man and put him in the Garden of Eden to work it and take care of it.

Genesis 2:15

> Thank you, creator God, for giving us an amazing world. Please show us how we can help take care of it with you. Amen.

 Try this!

Have fun working outdoors while enjoying God's beautiful world. Rake leaves in your yard or to help a neighbor. Maybe your church property or a park in your neighborhood needs helpers too. If it's not raking time in your area, grab a plastic bag and protective gloves and take a family walk, picking up litter along the way.

There's MORE to this story!

Read the WHOLE story in your Bible together! You can find it in the first book of the Old Testament: Genesis 2:4-25

In the Spark Story Bible, look for "Adam and Eve" on page 12.

The First Sin

God created a special place for Adam and Eve to walk with God. It was called the Garden of Eden. Adam and Eve were God's helpers in caring for everything in the garden. "Hisssssss"—a serpent tricked them into eating fruit from the one tree God had told them not to touch. God was heartbroken. Adam and Eve had to leave the garden. God still loved them and already had an incredible plan for them to be near God again, like they had been in the garden.

What happens when you make bad choices? Who helps you make good choices?

Key Verse

But the LORD God called to the man, "Where are you?"

Genesis 3:9

DEAR GOD, help us make good choices. Thank you for loving us when life is hard. Amen.

 Try this!

Make a paper chain snake with strips of construction paper. Put eyes and a tongue on one end for the head. Make the snake as long as you want. Each day tell about a good choice you made and remove a link. Can your family make the snake disappear?

📖 **There's MORE to this story!**

Read the WHOLE story in your Bible together! You can find it in the first book of the Bible: Genesis 3:1-24

In the Spark Story Bible, look for "The First Sin" on page 18.

Noah's Ark

When God told Noah to build a giant boat, Noah listened. It didn't look like a flood was coming, but Noah obeyed God. He built an ark and put many animals, two of every kind, inside to keep them safe. Because he trusted and obeyed God, Noah, his family, and the animals were saved from a flood that lasted 40 days and 40 nights!

Whom do you trust? When have you listened to God?

Key Verse

I have set my rainbow in the clouds, and it will be the sign of the covenant between me and the earth.

Genesis 9:13

> **DEAR GOD, help us to always trust you, as Noah did! Amen.**

 Try this!

Spread a blue blanket on the ground and enjoy a picnic together. Pretend you're having a picnic on the ark! Include foods that might have been available in Noah's time, such as grapes, dates, cheese, and pita bread. Bring some favorite toy animals with you in honor of the animals on Noah's ark!

There's MORE to this story!

Read the WHOLE story in your Bible together! You can find it in the very first book of the Old Testament: Genesis 6–9

In the Spark Story Bible, look for "Noah's Ark" on page 24.

Abram's Call

When Abram was an old man, God called him to leave home and go to a new land. With his family and everything he owned, Abram followed God. The trip was long, hot, and dusty. When they arrived in the new land, God blessed Abram, and Abram's family praised God for being faithful and providing a wonderful new place for them to live.

What might God be calling YOU to do? Who helps you follow God?

Key Verse

The LORD had said to Abram, "Go from your country, your people and your father's household to the land I will show you."

Genesis 12:1

> As we leave home today, God, lead us along the way. Help us listen to your call, whether we are big or small! Amen.

✨ Try this!

Abram's family lived in tents, but not just when they went camping—all the time! Imagine what their life might have been like by having a family "camp in." Arrange sleeping bags or lots of blankets on the floor. Tell stories and eat snacks by flashlight. Try to use no other electricity or technology.

📖 There's MORE to this story!

Read the WHOLE story in your Bible together! You can find it in the very first book of the Old Testament: Genesis 12:1-9

In the Spark Story Bible, look for "Abram's Call" on page 30.

God's Promises to Abram

God promised to give Abram a big, BIG family and a place for them to live. The promise was so BIG that Abram wondered if it could be true. God showed Abram all the stars in the sky and said, "This is how many people will be in your family." Abram believed God's BIG promise! Along with the promise, God gave Abram and Sarai new names: Abraham and Sarah!

Who is in your family? How does God love your family?

Key Verse

He took him outside and said, "Look up at the sky and count the stars—if indeed you can count them." Then he said to him, "So shall your offspring be."

Genesis 15:5

DEAR GOD, thank you for giving us our family. Amen.

Try this!

Go outside at night together and search for stars and constellations. A constellation is a group of stars that, with the help of your imagination, looks like a picture of something else, such as a person, a dragon, or even a bear! With an adult, search the Internet for a constellation map to help guide you or use a star app on a smartphone or tablet.

There's MORE to this story!

Read the WHOLE story in your Bible together! You can find it in the first book in the Bible: Genesis 15:1-12, 17-18

In the Spark Story Bible, look for "God's Promises to Abram" on page 34.

Abraham and Sarah's Visitors

Abraham and Sarah were an old married couple. God had promised them a big family, but it seemed like it would never happen. One day, people they didn't know appeared in the distance. Visitors were coming! Abraham and Sarah waited. When the visitors arrived, the guests shared good news: Sarah would have a son! Sarah laughed when she heard the news. She was old and had waited a long time to have a baby.

When have you had to wait a long time? What do you like to do while you're waiting?

Key Verse

"Is anything too hard for the LORD? I will return to you at the appointed time next year, and Sarah will have a son."

Genesis 18:14

> **DEAR GOD, help us when we have to wait for something we need or want. Amen.**

 Try this!

Play a waiting game. Get a timer and designate a special "waiting" chair. One person sits in the chair and says, "I'm waiting for [name] to visit." Everyone answers, "How long can you wait?" Start the timer. The person "waiting" should stay quiet and still for as long as possible, while the other players make silly faces at them. Stop the timer when the waiting person starts to talk, giggle, or squirm. Give each person a turn to wait. Who is best at waiting?

There's MORE to this story!

Read the WHOLE story in your Bible together! You can find it in the first book in the Bible: Genesis 17:1-7, 15-16; 18:1-15; 21:1-7

In the Spark Story Bible, look for "Abraham and Sarah's Visitors" on page 38.

Rebekah and Isaac

God promised Abraham a big family, but he and his wife, Sarah, had only one son, Isaac. When Isaac grew up, Abraham sent a servant to find Isaac a wife. The servant traveled a long way to a town where people believed in God. He asked God for a sign to help him know God's plan, and then went to the town well to wait. The sign from God came! A woman named Rebekah offered the servant water. She would be Isaac's wife.

When do you talk to God? What do you ask God?

Key Verse

He had the camels kneel down near the well outside the town; it was toward evening, the time the women go out to draw water.

Genesis 24:11

> **DEAR GOD, help us to wait with patience for your plan. Amen.**

 Try this!

Prepare a refreshing drink called *agua fresca* for visitors in your home. (*Agua fresca* is Spanish for "fresh water.") With adult help, puree about three cups of your favorite soft fruit. Strain the puree through a fine sieve to remove the pulp. Put juice in a pitcher and add about 1½ cups or more of plain or carbonated water. Add sugar and lime juice to taste. Enjoy with a guest!

There's MORE to this story!

Read the WHOLE story in your Bible together! You can find it in the first book of the Old Testament: Genesis 24; 25:19-28

In the Spark Story Bible, look for "Rebekah and Isaac" on page 42.

Isaac's Blessing

Even though they were twins, Jacob and Esau were exact opposites. They didn't look alike or act alike. When their father, Isaac, was old, Jacob tricked Isaac into giving him a special blessing that made him leader of the family instead of Esau.

How are your family members different? How are they the same?

Key Verse

Esau said to his father, "Do you have only one blessing, my father? Bless me too, my father!" Then Esau wept aloud.

Genesis 27:38

DEAR GOD, we are the same in some ways and different in others. That's how you made us. Help us work together.

Try this!

In today's story, Jacob prepared Esau a meal of lentil stew and bread. Pretend you are in the story, and make lentil stew (or soup) for your family.

It's yummy and healthy! With an adult, look online for an easy lentil soup recipe. Choose a recipe, and enjoy working together to make a meal for each other. Everyone can do different jobs, but it all comes together in the end.

There's MORE to this story!

Read the WHOLE story in your Bible together! You can find it in the first book in the Bible: Genesis 25:19-34; 27:1-40

In the Spark Story Bible, look for "Isaac's Blessing" on page 46.

Joseph and His Brothers

Joseph's family had problems! Joseph's father, Jacob, treated Joseph differently than his other sons. Jacob gave Joseph a colorful coat, which made the brothers angry. Joseph had dreams that made him think he was better than his brothers. God loved them all, but they forgot to love each other.

How does your family bother or frustrate you? What do you love about your family?

Key Verse

When his brothers saw that their father loved him more than any of them, they hated him and could not speak a kind word to him.

Genesis 37:4

> GOD OF PEACE, help us know that we need each other. Amen.

Try this!

When Joseph's brothers heard about his dreams, they rolled their eyes at his silliness. "OOOOOHHHH brother!" Pretend to be Joseph's brothers and hold an eye-rolling contest with your family.

Who can roll their eyes the fastest or the highest? What tall tales can you tell to make others roll their eyes?

There's MORE to this story!

Read the WHOLE story in your Bible together! You can find it in the first book of the Old Testament: Genesis 37:1-28

In the Spark Story Bible, look for "Joseph and His Brothers" on page 50.

Pharaoh's Dreams

Joseph had many hard times. His brothers sold him to a group of people traveling through their land. He was taken to Egypt, away from his family, and ended up in jail! While he was in jail, he helped two other prisoners understand their dreams. When the pharaoh had a dream he didn't understand, he asked Joseph for help. God helped Joseph understand Pharaoh's dream. Pharaoh was very thankful for Joseph's help and saw that he was very wise, so he made Joseph a leader over Egypt.

> What is one of the strangest dreams you've had? Do you think God still speaks to us through dreams?

Key Verse

"I cannot do it," Joseph replied to Pharaoh, "but God will give Pharaoh the answer he desires."

Genesis 41:16

> # GOD, thank you for taking care of Joseph! Thank you for taking care of me too!

⭐ Try this!

Make dream journals from scrap paper. Using a hole punch, make holes on the left side of a stack of paper. Bind the pages together using a colorful piece of yarn. Keep the journal near your bedside and write down your dreams. In the morning, share your dreams with your family while you eat breakfast. Is God saying anything to you?

📖 There's MORE to this story!

Read the WHOLE story in your Bible together! You can find it in the first book of the Bible: Genesis 39:20—41:57.

In the Spark Story Bible, look for "Pharaoh's Dreams" on page 56.

Joseph Helps His Family

Joseph hadn't seen his family in a long time. He was now a leader in Egypt, helping Pharaoh make decisions. People all over the region didn't have enough food to eat. God took care of Joseph. God told Joseph in a dream to prepare for the famine so that Egypt had enough food. Joseph's brothers heard there was food in Egypt. So they asked Joseph for help. Joseph's brothers had not been kind to him, but Joseph forgave them and helped them!

How does it feel to ask for forgiveness? How does it feel to forgive someone?

Key Verse

But Joseph said to them, "Don't be afraid. Am I in the place of God? You intended to harm me, but God intended it for good to accomplish what is now being done, the saving of many lives."

Genesis 50:19-20

> **FORGIVING GOD, help us forgive each other and love each other. Amen.**

Try this!

Create a family story comic book! Get a blank notebook and divide it into squares and rectangles. Use the pages to draw, color, and write about your favorite family stories. Just like Joseph's story, make sure to include lots of dramatic twists and turns! Every family member can contribute. Keep the book and add more stories as different things happen in your family life.

There's MORE to this story!

Read the WHOLE story in your Bible together! You can find it in the beginning of the Bible: Genesis 45:1-15; 50:15-21

In the Spark Story Bible, look for "Joseph Helps His Family" on page 62.

Baby Moses

The Hebrews were afraid. Pharaoh, the king of Egypt, ordered that Hebrew baby boys be drowned! One mom had a plan. She put her baby, Moses, in a basket and floated it down the Nile River. Moses' sister, Miriam, watched where the basket went. An amazing thing happened! Pharaoh's daughter found the basket and cared for the baby. God kept Moses safe.

How is floating fun or scary? What makes you feel safe?

Key Verse

When the child grew older, she took him to Pharaoh's daughter and he became her son. She named him Moses, saying, "I drew him out of the water."

Exodus 2:10

> GOD, Moses' mom trusted you to keep Moses safe. Help us to trust you too. Amen.

 Try this!

Baby Moses' mom put him in a basket made of papyrus reeds because she knew the basket would float and not sink. You can perform a sink-or-float experiment. Fill a large bowl or dishpan with water and gather objects that can get wet safely: coin, paper clip, plastic spoon, metal spoon, rock, cork, bath toy, and so on. Predict if an object will sink or float. Then drop the object in the water. Were you right?

There's MORE to this story!

Read the WHOLE story in your Bible together! You can find it in the second book in the Bible: Exodus 2:1-10

In the Spark Story Bible, look for "Baby Moses" on page 68.

The Burning Bush

When Moses was all grown up, he was watching his sheep when he saw flames coming from a bush. Then he heard God calling his name! "Tell Pharaoh to let my people go," God said. Moses was scared to do such a big job; no one was allowed to tell Pharaoh what to do. But God promised to be with him. Moses trusted God and did what God asked.

When have you done something hard? Who was with you?

Key Verse

And God said, "I will be with you. And this will be
the sign to you that it is I who have sent you: When
you have brought the people out of Egypt, you will
worship God on this mountain."

Exodus 3:12

> **GOD, thank you for being with us
> and for lighting our way! Amen.**

 Try this!

The Hebrew word for bush is *seneh*, which can also mean "brambles."
Brambles are prickly vines or shrubs. You can plant your own brambles!
Raspberry bushes are a great choice. If you don't have garden space,
look for a variety that thrives in containers. When you harvest the
bright red berries, retell the story of Moses and the burning bush.

There's MORE to this story!

Read the WHOLE story in your Bible together! You can find it in
the second book of the Old Testament: Exodus 3:1-15

In the Spark Story Bible, look for "The
Burning Bush" on page 74.

Free from Slavery

Moses' people, the Israelites, were slaves in Egypt. They had to work very hard and weren't treated very well. God told Moses he would help them escape, so Moses and his brother Aaron said to Pharaoh, "Our God says, 'Let my people go!'" Pharaoh would not listen. He refused to free them. But God wouldn't give up. God told Moses to try again. Moses was worried, but he knew God would win in the end, so he didn't give up either.

When have you stood up to a bully? How does God help you when you are worried?

Key Verse

"Therefore, say to the Israelites: 'I am the Lord, and I will bring you out from under the yoke of the Egyptians. I will free you from being slaves to them, and I will redeem you with an outstretched arm and with mighty acts of judgment.'"

Exodus 6:6

> MIGHTY GOD, I want to stand up to people who are unkind to others. Help me be brave. Amen.

 Try this!

Slavery and unfair working conditions are a reality around our world, even today. As a family, do some research about slavery in the supply chain for a common food item, like chocolate or coffee. Pray together about how you should respond. Ask God what you should do. Research practical ways you can stand up to these injustices and pick something to do as a family.

There's MORE to this story!

Read the WHOLE story in your Bible together! You can find it in the second book of the Old Testament: Exodus 5:1—6:13

In the Spark Story Bible, look for "Free from Slavery" on page 78.

41

The Plagues

God gave Moses a big message for Pharaoh: Let the Hebrew people go! But Pharaoh wouldn't listen. So God sent ten plagues to get Pharaoh's attention. Frogs, gnats, flies, and locusts swarmed the land! One frog is small, but thousands crowded Pharaoh's palace. One locust is tiny, but a cloud of them devoured Egypt's crops. Pharaoh couldn't ignore Moses' message any longer!

Who listens to you? When have you done a big job?

Key Verse

This is what the LORD says: By this you will know that I am the LORD: With the staff that is in my hand I will strike the water of the Nile, and it will be changed into blood.

Exodus 7:17

> GOD, help me listen for the message you have for me. Amen.

Try this!

Put a penny in a jar. The next day, put in two pennies. On the third day, put in three pennies; on the fourth put in four. Continue adding each day. How many days can you keep adding to the jar? When the jar is full, take it to a bank or coin exchange machine and convert the pennies to cash. As a family, decide on a charity and donate the money. Just like Moses, your little pennies can make a big difference!

There's MORE to this story!

Read the WHOLE story in your Bible together! You can find it in the second book in the Old Testament: Exodus 7:14—12:32

In the Spark Story Bible, look for "The Plagues" on page 80.

The Red Sea

Pharaoh finally agreed to free the Israelites, but after they left, he changed his mind. He took his army to find them and bring them back to Egypt. As Pharaoh's chariots charged closer, the Israelites got frightened. They were right next to the Red Sea and had nowhere else to go. "Stand firm," Moses said. "God is with us." Then Moses lifted up his staff. God parted the sea—and the people escaped to freedom!

What scares you? When have you been brave?

Key Verse

The LORD will fight for you; you need only to be still.

Exodus 14:14

> **Lead us forward, God. Help us to bravely follow you! Amen.**

🐸 Try this!

Moses and the Israelites camped on the shore of the Red Sea. In honor of them, pitch a tent and spend a night outdoors! Do some stargazing and cooking over a fire. If there is water nearby, try your hand at fishing or swimming, just like the ancient Israelites might have done.

📖 There's MORE to this story!

Read the WHOLE story in your Bible together! You can find it in the second book of the Old Testament: Exodus 14:1-30

In the Spark Story Bible, look for "The Red Sea" on page 86.

Manna, Quail, and Water

God promised Moses and the Israelites, God's people, a special home. Getting there wasn't easy! Kids were hungry, thirsty, and grouchy. God heard their complaints and sent quail for meat and manna for bread. When they needed water, God told Moses to hit a rock, and water came gushing out! God always provided just enough for every day.

What does hunger feel like? Where does your food come from?

Key Verse

"I have heard the grumbling of the Israelites. Tell them, 'At twilight you will eat meat, and in the morning you will be filled with bread. Then you will know that I am the LORD your God.'"

Exodus 16:12

✨ Try this!

God took care of the Israelites by providing enough food and water every day. Some kids in our world today don't have enough food to eat and clean water to drink. Collect non-perishable food items from your neighbors and friends and donate them to a local food bank. Your family could also volunteer to serve food at a community meal for people experiencing homelessness or pack food to send overseas.

📖 There's MORE to this story!

Read the WHOLE story in your Bible together! You can find it in the second book in the Old Testament: Exodus 16:1-18; 17:1-7

In the Spark Story Bible, look for "Manna, Quail, and Water" on page 92.

The Ten Commandments

God's people were on the long trip to the Promised Land, and they were having a hard time. God invited Moses to climb a mountain and talk. On the mountain, God gave Moses ten special rules, called commandments, to teach the people how to live together so life would be better for everyone. The commandments showed God's people how to love God and love each other.

How do you love God?
How do you love others?

Key Verse

I am the LORD your God, who brought you out of Egypt, out of the land of slavery.

Exodus 20:2

DEAR GOD, help us share your love with people we meet today. Be with us as we do our best. Amen.

 Try this!

The Ten Commandments were carved into stone tablets. It's hard to carve stone and hard to "erase" stone. Things that are "set in stone" are usually very important. Take a walk around your neighborhood looking for words and symbols carved in stone. Why is the carving you find important?

There's MORE to this story!

Read the WHOLE story in your Bible together! You can find it in Exodus, the second book of the Bible: Exodus 20:1-17

In the Spark Story Bible, look for "The Ten Commandments" on page 96.

The Battle of Jericho

The Israelites arrived at the land God promised, but tall walls protecting the city of Jericho stood in their way. Joshua led the Israelites in God's plan: They marched around the city for six days. Priests blew loud ram's horn trumpets called *shofars*, but the other marchers were completely silent. On the seventh day, they marched around the city seven times, and then the marchers shouted as loud as they could. SHAKE. CRUMBLE. CRASH. God brought the walls tumbling down!

When have you seen people marching? How do you praise God?

Key Verse

The seventh time around, when the priests sounded the trumpet blast, Joshua commanded the army, "Shout! For the LORD has given you the city!"

Joshua 6:16

> **MIGHTY GOD, you do great things! We shout our praise to you! Amen.**

 Try this!

The Israelites used instruments called shofars. You can make instruments out of things around your house: pots, pans, shakers made of plastic containers and dried beans, and toys that are musical instruments. With an adult, search the Internet for the song "Joshua Fit (or Fought) the Battle of Jericho." Play along with your new instruments.

There's MORE to this story!

Read the WHOLE story in your Bible together! You can find it in the first historical book in the Old Testament: Joshua 6:1-20

In the Spark Story Bible, look for "The Battle of Jericho" on page 102.

Deborah

The Israelites had been captured by their enemies! They prayed for help, and God responded by sending a woman named Deborah, who was a wise and faithful judge. Judges were important leaders chosen by God. "If you will trust God," Deborah said, "you can defeat your enemies." The Israelites listened to Deborah's message—and God helped them win their freedom!

When have you prayed to God? How has God helped you?

Key Verse

Then Deborah said to Barak, "Go! This is the day the LORD has given Sisera into your hands. Has not the LORD gone ahead of you?"

Judges 4:14a

Thank you, God, for helping me be brave
when I feel scared. I trust you! Amen.

Try this!

After being captured by enemies, the Israelites fought to win
their freedom. Remind yourselves of their story with the game
Capture the Flag! Look on the Internet or in a game book for
rules, and invite some friends to join you. Celebrate
afterward with fruit, cheese, crackers, and juice.

There's MORE to this story!

Read the WHOLE story in your Bible
together! You can find it in the seventh
book of the Bible: Judges 4:1—5:31

In the Spark Story Bible, look for
"Deborah" on page 107.

Naomi and Ruth

Naomi had two sons. They were married to Orpah and Ruth. Sadly, Naomi's sons died. Naomi wanted to move to the place where she grew up. She told Orpah and Ruth to stay with their people and find new husbands. Orpah went home, but Ruth stayed with Naomi until the end of the journey. They started a new life together.

How did Ruth show love? How do you show love to your family?

Key Verse

But Ruth replied, "Don't urge me to leave you or to turn back from you. Where you go I will go, and where you stay I will stay. Your people will be my people and your God my God."

Ruth 1:16

> **DEAR GOD, you gave us families to love. Thank you! Keep us safe on our journey as a family.**

✨💩 Try this!

Walk around your home with a camera. Take pictures of things that mean "family" to you. The things may include a special picture on the wall or a board game you play as a family. Don't forget to take pictures of people! Print the pictures and make a collage around the word "FAMILY" on poster board. God loves your family!

📖 There's MORE to this story!

Read the WHOLE story in your Bible together! You can find it in the book with the same name as one of this story's characters: Ruth 1:1-22

In the Spark Story Bible, look for "Naomi and Ruth" on page 110.

Ruth and Boaz

Ruth was Naomi's daughter-in-law. Both women's husbands had died, and they were very poor. Ruth worked hard to gather food for Naomi and herself. Naomi's relative, Boaz, saw how hard Ruth worked to take care of Naomi. He helped Ruth by giving her a place to get food and water.

How does your family get food?
How do you help your family?

Key Verse

May the LORD repay you for what you have done. May you be richly rewarded by the LORD, the God of Israel, under whose wings you have come to take refuge.

Ruth 2:12

DEAR GOD, thank you for our food. Help families who don't have enough to eat. Amen.

✨ Try this!

Some people today need help getting enough healthy food for their families. Many communities have food pantries where people can get food to feed their families. Take a trip to the grocery store with your family, purchase some of your favorite foods, and then donate them to your local food pantry. You'll be helping to make life easier for another family.

📖 There's MORE to this story!

Read the WHOLE story in your Bible together! You can find it in the Old Testament book named after Ruth: Ruth 2:1-17

In the Spark Story Bible, look for "Ruth and Boaz" on page 114.

57

Hannah Prays for a Child

Hannah wanted a child more than anything else. She waited for years. She prayed and prayed. One day a priest named Eli watched Hannah pray at the temple. He said God would answer her prayer. Hannah trusted God, and soon she had a baby boy! The baby, Samuel, grew up to be a servant of God in the temple with Eli, who had prophesied his birth!

When have you prayed for something for a long time? Who can you pray for?

Key Verse

I prayed for this child, and the LORD has granted me what I asked of him.

1 Samuel 1:27

> GOD, thank you for hearing our prayers every day. Amen.

 Try This!

Do you know anyone who has a new baby or is expecting a baby to come soon? Say a prayer for them today! Make a gift basket to support the new baby. Fill it with diapers, onesies, books, and baby toys—or even some snacks for the new parents. Bring it to the parents and let them know how excited you are about their child. As a family, you could even offer to babysit! Babies are a blessing from God.

There's MORE to this story!

Read the WHOLE story in your Bible together! You can find it in the first of two books named for Samuel, the son Hannah prayed for: 1 Samuel 1:9-27

In the Spark Story Bible, look for "Hannah Prays for a Child" on page 118.

God Calls Samuel

A boy named Samuel lived with an old priest named Eli. One night, Samuel heard someone call his name. Samuel ran to Eli. "Did you call me?" "No," Eli answered. "Go back to sleep!" The same thing happened again, and again. Finally Eli understood. "God is calling you, Samuel. The next time you hear him, tell God you are ready to listen." And Samuel did.

Who calls your name? When are you ready to listen?

Key Verse

The LORD came and stood there, calling as at the other times, "Samuel! Samuel!" Then Samuel said, "Speak, for your servant is listening."

1 Samuel 3:10

> DEAR GOD, Thank you for speaking to us. Help us to listen for your voice. Amen.

 Try this!

God surprised Samuel by calling his name in the night. Go outside after dark with an adult and listen to night sounds. Be as quiet as a mouse, and try to identify at least five different sounds. Come back inside and talk about what you heard while you enjoy a bedtime snack. Are night sounds scarier than day sounds? Why or why not?

There's MORE to this story!

Read the WHOLE story in your Bible together! You can find it in the first book named after the boy in the story: 1 Samuel 3:1-20

In the Spark Story Bible, look for "God Calls Samuel" on page 122.

David Is Chosen

When Samuel was an old prophet, God told him to choose a new king. God told Samuel to take a horn filled with oil to Bethlehem and choose a king from among Jesse's sons. So Samuel walked to Bethlehem and found Jesse. He looked at each one of Jesse's sons. None of them seemed quite right, except for one—Jesse's youngest son, David, who was watching the sheep outside. He came in and God told Samuel, "Yes! This is the new king!" So Samuel anointed him with oil, proclaiming him the next king.

When have you been chosen for something special? How did it make you feel?

Key Verse

So Samuel took the horn of oil and anointed him in the presence of his brothers, and from that day on the Spirit of the LORD came powerfully upon David.

1 Samuel 16:13a

GOD, thank you for choosing me to be your child! Thank you for giving me your Spirit! Amen.

 Try this!

As a family, go on a scavenger hunt around your home to find as many kinds of oil as you can. Ask a parent to tell you how each kind of oil is used. If it's safe, ask if you can smell and feel the oil. Some oil you can even taste! Be careful—some oil is flammable and toxic. Look for these types of oil: olive oil, vegetable oil, car oil, essential oils, candle oil, hinge oil, hair oil, and so on.

There's MORE to this story!

Read the WHOLE story in your Bible together! You can find it in the first book named for the prophet Samuel: 1 Samuel 16:1-13

In the Spark Story Bible, look for "David is Chosen" on page 126.

David and Goliath

The Israelites were trapped on a mountainside, facing an enemy army and its biggest, strongest soldier, Goliath. "Who will fight me?" roared Goliath. "I will do it," young David said. "God will protect me." David launched a smooth stone through the air with his slingshot. Down went Goliath. Up went the shout of victory. Hooray for David, who trusted God!

Whom do you trust? Who trusts you?

Key Verse

"The LORD who rescued me from the paw of the lion and the paw of the bear will rescue me from the hand of this Philistine." Saul said to David, "Go, and the LORD be with you."

1 Samuel 17:37

> ### Help us to trust you, God, even when our fears are big. Amen.

Try this!

David hit his target: Goliath's forehead. How is your aim? Practice by laying a hula hoop on the floor, moving back several steps, and tossing small stuffed animals into the ring. Or go outside and toss a beanbag or ball through the hoop. Challenge yourself by moving farther from the target.

📖 There's MORE to this story!

Read the WHOLE story in your Bible together! You can find it in a book named for the prophet Samuel: 1 Samuel 17:4-11, 32-50

In the Spark Story Bible, look for "David and Goliath" on page 130.

Solomon Builds the Temple

God chose Solomon, the son of King David, to build a temple. Solomon wanted the temple to be a beautiful place for the people to come and worship God together. The builders used fancy, expensive materials. When the temple was finished, God and the people were very happy to have such a special place to be together.

Where do you worship? What do you like about the place where you worship?

Key Verse

The temple that King Solomon built for the LORD was sixty cubits long, twenty wide and thirty high.

1 Kings 6:2

> **DEAR GOD, help us feel close to you when we worship. Amen.**

⭐ Try this!

Since Bible times, people have built beautiful buildings for gathering together and worshipping God. What can you build? Gather a variety of building toys and have fun together seeing what you can create. Who can build the tallest structure? The longest? The strongest? For a real challenge, grab a deck of cards and try to build a "house" of playing cards.

📖 There's MORE to this story!

Read the WHOLE story in your Bible together! You can find it in the first of two books of Kings: 1 Kings 6

In the Spark Story Bible, look for "Solomon Builds the Temple" on page 136.

Elijah and the Widow

God's prophet Elijah was hungry.
"Grrrrrr," went his tummy. He met a sad
widow and her son. The widow gave Elijah
water but had no food to share. Elijah told
her that God would make a miracle! She
went to work. With only a tiny bit of flour
and oil, the widow made many loaves of
bread. God gave them all enough!

When have you been hungry?
When have you fed someone else?

Key Verse

For the jar of flour was not used up and the jug of oil did not run dry, in keeping with the word of the LORD spoken by Elijah.

1 Kings 17:16

DEAR GOD, you give us everything we need. Help us to share with others. Amen.

 Try this!

Look in your pantry and refrigerator and take an inventory. What food items do you have a lot of? What do you have only a little of? Choose a few ingredients and make a meal from them together. Will you have more than enough for your family? Invite someone to eat with you!

There's MORE to this story!

Read the WHOLE story in your Bible together! You can find it in the historical section of the Old Testament: 1 Kings 17:8-16

In the Spark Story Bible, look for "Elijah and the Widow" on page 140.

Elisha Feeds 100

Elisha was one of God's prophets. He gave people messages from God, and he helped people be closer to God. A man brought 20 loaves of bread to Elisha as an offering to God. Elisha told him to give the loaves to the hungry people. The man was surprised—100 people were waiting, and 20 loaves wouldn't be enough. Plus, he had planned to give the bread to God, not people. Elisha told the man that God would make sure there was enough for everyone. When we give gifts to people, we are giving to God! The man handed out the bread. Everyone ate until they were full, and there were leftovers!

When was the last time you were surprised? When was the last time you shared food with someone else?

Key Verse

But Elisha answered, "Give it to the people to eat. For this is what the LORD says: 'They will eat and have some left over.'"

2 Kings 4:43b

GOD, thank you for providing us with healthy food. Amen.

 Try this!

Barley, the grain used in the bread in this story, tastes a little nutty. Find a recipe for barley bread and work together to bake a loaf. Invite friends or neighbors, and share with them the freshly baked bread and the story of Elisha feeding 100 people.

There's MORE to this story!

Read the WHOLE story in your Bible together! You can find it in the historical section of the Old Testament: 2 Kings 4:42-44

In the Spark Story Bible, look for "Elisha Feeds 100" on page 144.

73

Naaman Is Healed

Naaman was in charge of a large army. He was big, strong, and important. But he had a disease called leprosy, which gave him painful sores on his body. He heard about a prophet named Elisha who could heal him. So he decided to go see him. Before he arrived, he received a message from Elisha telling him that if he washed seven times in the river, he would be healed. How could this be? Naaman had taken lots of baths. He didn't understand how taking a bath in this river could be any different. But he did what Elisha said. It worked! God healed Naaman.

> When was the last time you were sick? What made you feel better?

Key Verse

So he went down and dipped himself in the Jordan seven times, as the man of God had told him, and his flesh was restored and became clean like that of a young boy.

2 Kings 5:14

DEAR GOD, you are a great healer! Thank you for helping me feel better when I am sick.

Try this!

Do you know anyone who is sick? Make them a care package to help them feel better. Fill it with cans of chicken noodle soup, activities to do, books to read, pictures you drew, or anything else you can think of. As a family, deliver the package and let the person know you are praying for them.

There's MORE to this story!

Read the WHOLE story in your Bible together! You can find it in the historical section of the Old Testament: 2 Kings 5:1-19

In the Spark Story Bible, look for "Naaman is Healed" on page 148.

73

Queen Esther

Esther was a beautiful Jewish woman who became queen. Her cousin, Mordecai, lived in the city. Haman, a man who worked for the king, made some bad rules. Mordecai refused to follow them. This made Haman angry. He threatened to have all the Jewish people killed! Queen Esther was afraid the king would harm her too if she told him about Haman's plans. But she did the right thing and asked him for help, and the Jewish people were saved!

Who helps you when you're afraid? What helps you be brave?

Key Verse

Esther again pleaded with the king, falling at his feet and weeping. She begged him to put an end to the evil plan of Haman the Agagite, which he had devised against the Jews.

Esther 8:3

> **MIGHTY GOD, give us the courage of Queen Esther when the right thing to do is difficult or scary. Amen.**

Try this!

One of the ways Jewish people celebrate the festival of Purim is to act out the story of Queen Esther. Get some of your family and friends together, and as you read the story in your Bible, act it out. Whenever the reader says the name Haman, everybody should respond with a loud and dramatic "Booo!" When the reader says the name Mordecai or Esther, everyone should cheer as loudly as they can.

There's MORE to this story!

Read the WHOLE story in your Bible together! You can find it in the book named for Queen Esther: Esther 2:5-18; 3:1-6; 8:1-17

In the Spark Story Bible, look for "Queen Esther" on page 153.

The Lord Is My Shepherd

David was a shepherd before he became king of Israel. Shepherds do a lot to take care of their sheep: they make sure that sheep have food to eat, have water to drink, and are safe from danger. The way David cared for sheep reminded him of the ways God cares for us, so he wrote a song about it. David knew God cared for him.

Who cares for you? How do you care for others?

Key Verse

The LORD is my shepherd, I lack nothing. He makes me lie down in green pastures, he leads me beside quiet waters, he refreshes my soul.

Psalm 23:1-3a

DEAR GOD, help me to know how much you care for me. Amen.

 Try this!

David wrote a lot of songs! You can too! Write a song about how God cares for you. Make up a tune or use a tune you already know. Have a family talent show and perform your songs for each other. Singing songs to God is a wonderful way to worship.

There's MORE to this story!

Read the WHOLE story in your Bible together! You can find it in the very middle of the Bible: Psalm 23

In the Spark Story Bible, look for "The Lord Is My Shepherd" on page 158.

A Child Called Immanuel

King Ahaz was about to make a BIG mistake. King Ahaz was about to go to war, but God wanted him to wait. God's messenger, Isaiah, warned Ahaz, and God gave Ahaz a sign to look for—a child named Immanuel. Ahaz didn't listen to God and went to war anyway. Many people died. But the people of Israel listened, remembered, and waited for the child to be born.

Who do you listen to? When is listening difficult? Why?

Key Verse

Therefore the LORD himself will give you a sign: The virgin will conceive and give birth to a son, and will call him Immanuel.

Isaiah 7:14

> **DEAR GOD, we are listening. Teach us, tell us, show us what YOU want us to do. Amen.**

Try this!

Buy or borrow a baby name book and have fun looking up the meanings of your name and names of family members and friends. Does the book have the meaning of the name Jesus? (Matthew 1:21 offers a hint!)

📖 There's MORE to this story!

Read the WHOLE story in your Bible together! You can find it in one of the books of the prophets in the Old Testament: Isaiah 7:10-17

In the Spark Story Bible, look for "A Child Called Immanuel" on page 162.

God's Peaceful World

Isaiah was a prophet. He told the people that God promised to send a child to bring peace to the world. The child would show people how to love God and love each other. When the child comes, even wolves and lambs will live in peace, he said.

What does peace feel like?
Is peace easy or hard? Why?

Key Verse

The wolf will live with the lamb, the leopard will lie down with the goat, the calf and the lion and the yearling together; and a little child will lead them.

Isaiah 11:6

> **GOD, sometimes peace is hard. Help us to love everyone, like you do, no matter what. Amen.**

Try this!

Send a peace letter or email to family and friends. Tell about what you have learned about peace. Ask that everyone respond with ideas about peace. Read the ideas together during family time.

There's MORE to this story!

Read the WHOLE story in your Bible together! You can find it in the last section of the Old Testament, the books of the prophets: Isaiah 11:1-10

In the Spark Story Bible, look for "God's Peaceful World" on page 166.

Fiery Furnace

King Nebuchadnezzar was mad! Shadrach, Meshach, and Abednego worshipped only God and refused to bow down to the king's huge gold statue of himself. The king ordered the men to be thrown into a hot furnace. It was very scary, but God protected them. The king could see four people in the furnace, even though he'd thrown only three men in! Shadrach, Meshach, and Abednego walked out of the furnace without any burns on their bodies! The king was amazed and knew that God was with them.

Key Verse

Then Nebuchadnezzar said, "Praise be to the God of Shadrach, Meshach and Abednego, who has sent his angel and rescued his servants! They trusted in him and defied the king's command and were willing to give up their lives rather than serve or worship any god except their own God."

Daniel 3:28

GOD, sometimes it is hard to do the right thing. Help us to trust you. Amen.

Try this!

Make a fiery furnace snack. Put graham crackers on a cookie sheet. Sprinkle chocolate chips and mini marshmallows on each cracker. Put three bear-shaped graham crackers on top. Pop them in the "fiery furnace" (375°F oven) for five minutes. The chocolate and marshmallows melt, but the bears are fine! Let them cool before eating. Talk about safety in your kitchen.

There's MORE to this story!

Read the WHOLE story in your Bible together! You can find it in the prophets section of the Old Testament: Daniel 3:19-30

In the Spark Story Bible, look for "Fiery Furnace" on page 170.

Daniel and the Lions

Daniel worshipped God. But the law said that everyone had to worship King Darius. Thump! Daniel was thrown in a pit of snarling lions because he would not worship the king. Daniel prayed, and the lions closed their toothy grins and rested their heads on their paws. In the morning, Daniel was still alive. King Darius was surprised! From that day, King Darius believed in God.

When are you scared? Who do you turn to for comfort?

Key Verse

[God] rescues and he saves; he performs signs and wonders in the heavens and on the earth. He has rescued Daniel from the power of the lions.

Daniel 6:27

> GOD, thank you for keeping us safe through the dark of the night. Amen.

 Try this!

Talk together about scary times. How do we know God is with us? "He's Got the Whole World in His Hands" is a favorite song about how God cares for the world. Sing the song together. If you need the lyrics, do an Internet search with adult help. The next time you are scared, you can sing the song to yourself.

There's MORE to this story!

Read the WHOLE story in your Bible together! You can find it in the book named for the man in this story: Daniel 6:1-28

In the Spark Story Bible, look for "Daniel and the Lions" on page 174.

Jonah and the Big Fish

God told Jonah to go to a city called Nineveh (NIH-neh-veh). Jonah disobeyed. He got on a boat and went the other way. During a terrible storm, Jonah was thrown into the ocean and was swallowed by a BIG fish! Jonah prayed to God for help— and was rescued. Then Jonah listened to God. He went to Nineveh to tell the people how God wanted them to live.

When are you reluctant to do what God says? How does it feel to do the right thing?

Key Verse

In my distress I called to the LORD, and he answered me. From deep in the realm of the dead I called for help, and you listened to my cry.

Jonah 2:2

> **DEAR GOD, help us to listen to you wisely, wherever we are and whatever we do! Amen.**

Try this!

God told Jonah to visit the city of Nineveh, but Jonah went the other way. Nineveh was the capital of the country of Assyria. It had over 120,000 people! Go for a walk in a city near you. Can you imagine how your modern city would compare with ancient Nineveh? Bring along some fish-shaped crackers for a snack to remember what happened to Jonah.

There's MORE to this story!

Read the WHOLE story in your Bible together! You can find it toward the end of the Old Testament: Jonah 1–4

In the Spark Story Bible, look for "Jonah and the Big Fish" on page 180.

A Ruler from Bethlehem

The people of Bethlehem felt scared and hopeless because disaster was coming to their city. Then God's messenger, Micah, shared good news: the greatest leader the world had ever seen would be born in Bethlehem! This leader would care for all people, especially those who need extra help. The message gave the people hope!

Who are your leaders? What makes a leader great?

Key Verse

He will stand and shepherd his flock in the strength of the LORD, in the majesty of the name of the Lord his God. And they will live securely, for then his greatness will reach to the ends of the earth.

Micah 5:4

GOD, help leaders in our country, church, school, workplace, neighborhood, and home to make wise choices. Amen.

Try this!

Sing Christmas carols that mention Bethlehem, such as "O Little Town of Bethlehem," "Hark! The Herald Angels Sing," or "O Come, All Ye Faithful." What do these songs say about Bethlehem? About God and Jesus? Sing some of these songs together and go caroling!

There's MORE to this story!

Read the WHOLE story in your Bible together! You can find it near the end of the Old Testament: Micah 5:2-5

In the Spark Story Bible, look for "A Ruler from Bethlehem" on page 184.

Angels Visit

Mary and Joseph were engaged to be married. An angel told Mary she was going to have a baby—God's Son! Mary was amazed. Joseph didn't believe it at first, but an angel spoke to him in a dream. Joseph was amazed too. They decided to marry and name the baby Jesus.

What amazes you? What is amazing about God?

Key Verse

"I am the Lord's servant," Mary answered. "May your word to me be fulfilled." Then the angel left her.

Luke 1:38

 Try this!

What do angels look like? No one really knows, but in the Bible, when God sent angels to earth, they often took on human form. Have fun making different kinds of angels—paper cutouts, angel ornaments to decorate your home, cookie angels to eat or give as gifts, and if the weather is right, snow angels!

There's MORE to this story!

Read the WHOLE story in your Bible together! You can find it in two of the Gospel books: Matthew 1:18-25; Luke 1:26-38

In the Spark Story Bible, look for "Angels Visit" on page 186.

Mary Visits Elizabeth

Mary was a young girl. Her relative Elizabeth was an older woman. They were both going to have the babies that God had promised them. Mary went to visit Elizabeth, and when Elizabeth saw Mary, her own baby jumped with excitement inside of her! Mary sang a joyful song of praise to God. God had blessed Mary and Elizabeth.

When do you feel blessed?
How do you praise God?

Key Verse

For the Mighty One has done great things for me—holy is his name.

Luke 1:49

GOD, we praise you! You keep your promises. Thank you for blessing us. Amen.

Try this!

The song of praise Mary sang when she visited Elizabeth is called the *Magnificat*, because the first line says, "My soul magnifies the Lord." On a large sheet of paper, write or draw special things about God and great things God has done in your family. Using these ideas, create your own family praise song set to a well-known tune.

There's MORE to this story!

Read the WHOLE story in your Bible together! You can find it in the third book of the New Testament: Luke 1:39-58

In the Spark Story Bible, look for "Mary Visits Elizabeth" on page 192.

Jesus Is Born

Mary and Joseph had to go on a long trip to the city of Bethlehem. It was not easy to travel because Mary was still pregnant. When they finally arrived in Bethlehem, Jesus was born! Angels told shepherds about Jesus, and the shepherds traveled to see the baby. When they left Mary, Joseph, and baby Jesus, they couldn't stop talking about how awesome it was to see the Son of God! They praised God for the chance to see such an amazing miracle.

How do you celebrate a new baby?
How do you celebrate Jesus' birth?

Key Verse

Today in the town of David a Savior has been born to you; he is the Messiah, the Lord. This will be a sign to you: You will find a baby wrapped in cloths and lying in a manger.

Luke 2:11-12

> **GOD, thank you for babies. Most of all, thank you for baby Jesus! Amen.**

Try this!

Tell the story of Jesus' birth with a family Christmas pageant. Make sure every family member gets a part. Make costumes and use props from around your home. Have someone record a video or take photos of your Christmas play.

📖 There's MORE to this story!

Read the WHOLE story in your Bible together! You can find it in the third book of the New Testament: Luke 2:1-20

In the Spark Story Bible, look for "Jesus Is Born" on page 198.

Wise Men

Wise men were waiting for an important person to come into the world. When they saw a bright star in the sky, they knew it was the sign from God that they were waiting for. They followed the star to baby Jesus. The wise men gave Jesus gifts and worshipped him. God gave the whole world the gift of Jesus, the wise men gave Jesus special gifts, and today many people choose to continue this tradition by giving gifts to one another when they celebrate Jesus' birth!

> How does it feel to give a gift?
> How does it feel to get a gift?

Key Verse

On coming to the house, they saw the child with his mother Mary, and they bowed down and worshiped him. Then they opened their treasures and presented him with gifts of gold, frankincense and myrrh.

Matthew 2:11

DEAR GOD, thank you for giving us the gift of your son Jesus! Amen.

Try this!

All babies are special, and all babies need things to help them stay healthy and happy. Sometimes families with new babies have a hard time. Food shelves, crisis nurseries, and other organizations work to help these families. Find out if your church works with one of these types of organizations or contact one directly to find out what families need most. Put together a special gift for a baby and his or her family with things the baby needs, such as diapers, wipes, formula, and baby soap and lotion.

There's MORE to this story!

Read the WHOLE story in your Bible together! You can find it in the first book in the New Testament: Matthew 2:1-12

In the Spark Story Bible, look for "Wise Men" on page 204.

Simeon and Anna

Simeon and Anna loved God. They were prophets who lived in the Temple. They waited a long time to see who God was sending to save the world. Mary and Joseph brought baby Jesus to the Temple. When Simeon and Anna saw him, they knew Jesus was special. They praised God for Jesus!

When have you had to wait a long time for something? How did you feel when the wait was over?

Key Verse

[Simeon said,] "For my eyes have seen your salvation, which you have prepared in the sight of all nations."

Luke 2:30-31

GOD, we praise you! We celebrate Jesus' coming into our world. Amen.

 Try this!

Look online to see how others praise God all around the world. Pay attention for new languages, new kinds of dancing, and new music. Praise God by making a video of your own to share!

There's MORE to this story!

Read the WHOLE story in your Bible together! You can find it in the third book of the New Testament: Luke 2:22–40

In the Spark Story Bible, look for "Simeon and Anna" on page 210.

The Boy at the Temple

Jesus' family went on a trip every year to the Temple in Jerusalem. The family walked there with many other people. On one of these trips, when Jesus was 12 years old, Mary and Joseph couldn't find Jesus. They were afraid he was lost! They finally found him—he was in the Temple telling people about God.

How does your family make sure that everyone is safe on a trip? What would you do if you were lost?

Key Verse

"Why were you searching for me?" he asked. "Didn't you know I had to be in my Father's house?"

Luke 2:49

> **GOD, thank you for keeping us safe when we go on trips. Help us not to be afraid when we feel lost.**

Try this!

Take a family walk every day this week. Record how far you walked each day and try to increase a little every day. At the end of the week, add up your numbers to calculate your total distance. Do you think you walked as far as Jesus' family?

There's MORE to this story!

Read the WHOLE story in your Bible together! You can find it in one of the Gospels. *Gospel* means "good news": Luke 2:41–52

In the Spark Story Bible, look for "The Boy at the Temple" on page 214.

John the Baptist

John the Baptist was Jesus' cousin. God gave him an important job: to tell people that Jesus was coming! John stood by a river, teaching, preaching, and baptizing people. "Jesus is coming! He will save us all!" John shouted. Some people didn't listen. But many people believed John and were ready for Jesus.

How do you learn about Jesus? Who teaches you about Jesus?

Key Verse

As it is written in Isaiah the prophet: "I will send my messenger ahead of you, who will prepare your way"—"a voice of one calling in the wilderness, 'Prepare the way for the Lord, make straight paths for him.'"

Mark 1:2-3

> GOD, thank you for all the people who tell us about Jesus. Amen.

 Try this!

John's job was to tell others about Jesus. Interview your pastor or someone else whose job is to teach others about Jesus. Grab a notebook and pencil or a video or audio recorder. Here are some questions to get you started:

When did you know you wanted to be in ministry?
What subjects did you study in school?
What is your favorite part of your job?

There's MORE to this story!

Read the WHOLE story in your Bible together! You can find it in all four Gospels: Matthew 11:2-11; Mark 1:1-8; Luke 3:1-18; John 1:6-8, 19-28

In the Spark Story Bible, look for "John the Baptist" on page 218.

Jesus' Baptism

John baptized people who wanted to change their lives and follow God. He also said someone was coming who would change the world. One day his cousin Jesus asked to be baptized. When Jesus came up out of the water, the Holy Spirit appeared in the form of a dove, and a voice said, "This is my Son. He is beloved and chosen!"

What do you know about baptism? Who do you know who has been baptized?

Key Verse

[John said,] "I baptize you with water for repentance. But after me comes one who is more powerful than I, whose sandals I am not worthy to carry. He will baptize you with the Holy Spirit and fire."

Matthew 3:11

GOD, thank you for sending Jesus and marking him and us with your love. Amen.

⭐ Try this!

Take time as a family to go on a walk near a body of water close to your home—an ocean, a lake, a river, a stream, a pond, or even a mud puddle. What lives in and around the water? Why is this water important? How do this water and this place change with the seasons?

📖 There's MORE to this story!

Read the WHOLE story in your Bible together! You can find it in the first three books in the New Testament: Matthew 3:13-17; Mark 1:4-11; Luke 3:15-17, 21-22

In the Spark Story Bible, look for "Jesus' Baptism" on page 224.

Jesus Goes to Nazareth

Jesus was teaching at the synagogue in his hometown, Nazareth. He told the people, "God loves everyone—even people who are poor, people who are sick, and people who are in jail." But the people listening didn't agree. "Go away!" they told Jesus. Jesus left, but he kept showing and telling people that God's love is for everyone.

Who loves you? How do you show love?

Key Verse

The Spirit of the Lord is on me, because he has anointed me to proclaim good news to the poor. He has sent me to proclaim freedom for the prisoners and recovery of sight for the blind, to set the oppressed free, to proclaim the year of the Lord's favor.

Luke 4:18-19

> **LOVING GOD, thank you for loving me. Help me to share your love with someone today. Amen.**

Try this!

Jesus read God's Word from the scroll of Isaiah. You can share God's love with a scroll too! Cut a long strip of paper. Crush it to make it look old. Write a message about God's love (a favorite Bible verse or your own words). Roll it up, tie it with ribbon, and give it to someone who would like to hear the message.

📖 There's MORE to this story!

Read the WHOLE story in your Bible together! You can find it in the third Gospel: Luke 4:14-30

In the Spark Story Bible, look for "Jesus Goes to Nazareth" on page 228.

Jesus Heals

People everywhere heard that Jesus was a healer. They brought their sick family and friends to Jesus so he could heal them. One morning, Jesus' friend Simon Peter asked him to heal his wife's mother. "She has a terrible fever. I know you've healed other people. Can you heal her too?" he asked. Jesus went to the woman and healed her.

When was the last time you were sick? What made you feel better?

Key Verse

The whole town gathered at the door, and Jesus healed many who had various diseases.

Mark 1:33-34a

HEALING GOD, thank you for being with me when I'm sick! Please heal the people I know who are sick. In Jesus' name, amen.

Try this!

Do you know anyone who is in the hospital or isn't feeling well? Find out if you can visit them. Bring them a card or flowers. You could even sing them a song or tell them a story to help them feel better.

There's MORE to this story!

Read the WHOLE story in your Bible together! You can find it the second book of the New Testament: Mark 1:29-39

In the Spark Story Bible, look for "Jesus Heals" on page 230.

The Disciples

Jesus called men and women to follow him and to help build God's kingdom. He asked fishermen to catch people instead of fish. He asked tax collectors to collect people instead of money. Lots of different people decided to give up their jobs and started helping Jesus spread God's love. Jesus chose 12 people to be his closest disciples, called *apostles*, and follow him wherever he went.

How do you follow Jesus? What would be hard to give up for Jesus?

Key Verse

These are the names of the twelve apostles: first, Simon (who is called Peter) and his brother Andrew; James son of Zebedee, and his brother John; Philip and Bartholomew; Thomas and Matthew the tax collector; James son of Alphaeus, and Thaddaeus; Simon the Zealot and Judas Iscariot, who betrayed him.

Matthew 10:2-4

> JESUS, we want to be your disciples and spread your Word in the world! Amen.

Try this!

Go "fishing" like some of the disciples. Lay out a blue blanket, get a large box or tub for a boat, and tie a string to a pole or stick. Sit in the "boat" and imagine what Jesus meant when he talked about "fishing" for people.

There's MORE to this story!

Read the WHOLE story in your Bible together! You can find it in two Gospel books: Matthew 4:12-23; 9:9-13; 10:1-4; Luke 5:1-11; 8:1-3

In the Spark Story Bible, look for "The Disciples" on page 232.

The Beatitudes

One day Jesus climbed a mountain and told a crowd about the people God blesses: people who feel hopeless, sad, and hurt; people who don't have a lot of things; people who want to follow God; kind people; people who know what is right in their heart; and people who make peace. This wasn't what people expected to hear! Jesus' message about the people God blesses is called the Beatitudes.

Who is a blessing to your family? How do you feel blessed?

Key Verse

Blessed are the peacemakers, for they will be called children of God.

Matthew 5:9

> Bless me, God, so I may be a blessing to others. Amen.

 Try this!

Does your family know someone who is sad, feels hopeless, or is hungry? Talk about how you could help this person and show that he or she is blessed by God. Put your words into action and come up with a specific plan to help.

There's MORE to this story!

Read the WHOLE story in your Bible together! You can find it in the first book of the New Testament: Matthew 5:1-12

In the Spark Story Bible, look for "The Beatitudes" on page 238.

Love Your Enemies

When Jesus taught people about God, he shared some surprising news: When someone hurts you, don't hurt them back. Help everyone. Share what you have with other people. Jesus told people that they should love everyone—friends *and* enemies. The people were so confused! God's love was a different kind of love than they had heard about before!

When is it easy to love someone?
When is it hard to love someone?

Key Verse

You have heard that it was said, "Love your neighbor and hate your enemy." But I tell you, love your enemies and pray for those who persecute you, that you may be children of your Father in heaven.

Matthew 5:43-45a

> **LOVING GOD, help us to love everyone we meet the way you love all of us. Amen.**

 Try this!

Loving others isn't always easy. As a family, role-play how you could respond in love to the following scenarios: A) Someone calls you a mean word on the playground. What do you do? B) It's your birthday and you're trying to decide whether or not to invite someone you don't like very much. What do you do? C) Your sibling is annoying you. What do you do?

There's MORE to this story!

Read the WHOLE story in your Bible together! You can find it in the first book of the New Testament: Matthew 5:38-48

In the Spark Story Bible, look for "Love Your Enemies" on page 242.

Do Not Worry

Jesus taught his followers not to worry because God takes care of everyone and everything. "Look at the birds, look at the flowers—they do not worry," Jesus said. "God takes care of them." We can put God first in our lives and trust God to take care of us.

What do you worry about? What helps you to stop worrying?

Key Verse

Therefore do not worry about tomorrow, for tomorrow will worry about itself. Each day has enough trouble of its own.

Matthew 6:34

GOD, help us not to worry. You take care of us wherever we go. Amen.

Try this!

Help birds not to worry about where they will get their food by making a simple bird feeder. With an adult, find a pinecone or empty toilet paper roll and a length of yarn or ribbon. Cover the pinecone or paper roll with a nut butter or honey and roll it in birdseed until it is covered with seed. If you use a pinecone, tie the yarn to the pinecone and then tie off a loop with the remainder. If you use a paper roll, thread the yarn through the tube and tie a knot. Hang it outside and watch what happens!

There's MORE to this story!

Read the WHOLE story in your Bible together! You can find it in the first Gospel in the New Testament: Matthew 6:24-34

In the Spark Story Bible, look for "Do Not Worry" on page 244.

The Lord's Prayer

Jesus' disciples wanted to learn how to pray. "Teach us," they said to Jesus. Jesus said that prayer is a time to focus on God and that using a loud voice or big words isn't important. Then Jesus gave the disciples a prayer. We call it "the Lord's Prayer," and we still pray it today.

> What do you know about prayer?
> What do you pray about?

Key Verse

He said to them, "When you pray, say: 'Father, hallowed be your name, your kingdom come. Give us each day our daily bread. Forgive us our sins, for we also forgive everyone who sins against us. And lead us not into temptation.'"

Luke 11:2-4

> **DEAR GOD, praying helps us grow close to you. Thank you for always listening. Amen.**

✨ Try this!

Keep a prayer journal by yourself or as a family. Think of it as writing a letter to God or drawing a picture for God. You can share all of your feelings with God: happy, sad, angry, confused, curious, or anything else you feel. God will always listen.

📖 There's MORE to this story!

Read the WHOLE story in your Bible together! You can find it in two Gospels: Matthew 6:5-15; Luke 11:1-10

In the Spark Story Bible, look for "The Lord's Prayer" on page 246.

House on the Rock

Jesus liked to teach people by telling stories. Here's one: Two people built houses. One house was built on a rock and the other on the sand. A bad storm came. The house on the sand crashed down, but the house on the rock stood strong. When you listen to Jesus, your life is built on the sturdy rock of God.

What's your favorite story to hear? What's your favorite story to tell?

Key Verse

[Jesus said,] "Everyone who hears these words of mine and puts them into practice is like a wise man who built his house on the rock."

Matthew 7:24

DEAR GOD, thank you for the stories Jesus told. Help us learn from these stories so that we can trust God ALL THE TIME! Amen.

Try this!

Use blocks to try to build a house of your own. Start with two blocks on the bottom and see how tall your house can be. Add more blocks to the bottom each time you build. Do more blocks at the base help you build the house taller? Why? Would sand be a good foundation for a building or block tower? Why or why not?

There's MORE to this story!

Read the WHOLE story in your Bible together! You can find it in the first book in the New Testament: Matthew 7:24-28

In the Spark Story Bible, look for "House on the Rock" on page 250.

121

Storm

The disciples were fishing when Jesus decided to take a nap in the boat. Rain started to fall. The wind blew hard! Waves splashed! Thunder clapped! "Wake up, Jesus!" the disciples cried. "Help us!" Jesus woke up and asked why they were scared. He commanded the storm to stop. The waves calmed. The rain stopped. The sun shined. The disciples were amazed at Jesus' power!

When was the last time you experienced a storm? How did it make you feel?

Key Verse

The disciples went and woke him, saying, "Lord, save us! We're going to drown!" He replied, "You of little faith, why are you so afraid?" Then he got up and rebuked the winds and the waves, and it was completely calm.

Matthew 8:25-26

THANK YOU, God, for being with us when scary things happen. Help us to have faith in you. Amen.

Try this!

Play a water game to help the disciples get from one side of the Sea of Galilee to the other side safely. Gather a straw for each person, a cork, and a large baking pan with sides and lots of towels (if you are playing inside) or a wading pool (if you are playing outside). Have an adult fill the pan or pool with water.

Pretend the cork is the boat with Jesus and the disciples. Taking turns, use a straw to blow the cork from one side to the other side. Other players may use straws to create scary "waves" and throw the boat off course. Cheer when the boat reaches the other side.

There's MORE to this story!

Read the WHOLE story in your Bible together! You can find it in the first New Testament book: Matthew 8:23-27

In the Spark Story Bible, look for "A Storm" on page 254.

123

The Centurion's Servant

A large crowd was waiting to see Jesus when a powerful soldier called a *centurion* appeared. Centurions usually did not get along with people like Jesus. But this centurion had faith that Jesus could heal his servant, who couldn't walk. "You are more powerful than I am," the centurion said to Jesus. The centurion was right—Jesus healed the servant right then, without even seeing him!

Key Verse

When Jesus heard this, he was amazed and said to those following him, "Truly I tell you, I have not found anyone in Israel with such great faith."

Matthew 8:10

LOVING GOD, please help me feel better when I'm sick. Amen.

 Try this!

Do you know anyone who is sick, injured, or sad about something in his or her life? Ask family members if they know anyone like this. Make a list of people who need prayers and add people to it each week. Pray for the people on the list with your family. If someone gets better, celebrate and thank God when you take them off the list!

📖 **There's MORE to this story!**

Read the WHOLE story in your Bible together! You can find it in the first book in the New Testament: Matthew 8:5-13

In the Spark Story Bible, look for "The Centurion's Servant" on page 258.

125

The Sower

Here's a story Jesus told: A farmer scattered seeds on the ground. Some seeds landed on a hard path, some seeds landed on rocks, and some landed in the weeds. These seeds didn't have a good place to grow, so they died. But some seeds landed in good soil, and these plants grew strong and healthy! God's Word grows in good soil.

What do seeds need to grow strong? What do you need to grow strong?

Key Verse

The seed falling on good soil refers to someone who hears the word and understands it. This is the one who produces a crop, yielding a hundred, sixty or thirty times what was sown.

Matthew 13:23

> GOD, help us grow in your Word! Amen.

 Try this!

Do a gardening experiment. Get some seeds for green beans and some paper cups. Fill the paper cups with different kinds of soil: rocky soil, sandy soil, and good black potting soil. Place one bean in each cup and cover it with another inch of soil. Water them and place the cups on a sunny windowsill. Watch what happens and record your observations each day. How long does it take for each bean to sprout? If you get healthy plants, move them to a bigger planter or a garden bed outside.

There's MORE to this story!

Read the WHOLE story in your Bible together! You can find it in the first book in the New Testament: Matthew 13:1-9, 18-23

In the Spark Story Bible, look for "The Sower" on page 260.

Walking on Water

As the disciples were fishing, they saw Jesus walking toward them—on top of the water! Peter stepped out of the boat to try walking on water too. But he was scared, and when he looked away from Jesus, Peter started to sink! Jesus helped Peter and asked him to trust. Peter and the disciples believed and told others about Jesus, God's Son.

When is it easy to trust? When is it hard?

Key Verse

Immediately Jesus reached out his hand and caught him. "You of little faith," he said, "why did you doubt?"

Matthew 14:31

> **DEAR JESUS, help me to always keep my eyes on you—not on my fears. Amen.**

Try this!

Draw a cross on the left side of an index card and a dot on the right side. Hold the card in your right hand at eye level. Cover your left eye and focus on the cross. Slowly move the card away from your face. What happens to the dot? Remember this: Focus on Jesus and fears disappear!

There's MORE to this story!

Read the WHOLE story in your Bible together! You can find it in the beginning of the New Testament: Matthew 14:22-33

In the Spark Story Bible, look for "Walking on Water" on page 262.

The Vineyard Workers

Jesus told a story about a farmer who hired workers to work in his vineyard. Some workers worked all day. Some worked half a day. Some worked just at the end of the day. The workers were surprised when the farmer paid everyone the same amount! God is like the generous farmer. God's love is BIG and includes everyone!

How does your family show love? How can you be generous with love?

Key Verse

[Jesus said,] "So the last will be first, and the first will be last."

Matthew 20:16

GOD, you are generous to us all the time. Show us how to be generous to someone today. Amen.

⭐ Try this!

Practice some math to make number sentences that are equal. Get a deck of cards with the face cards and jokers removed. Choose a number between 10 and 20. Use the cards to create addition sentences that equal your chosen number. Can you use more than two cards to get to your target number?

📖 There's MORE to this story!

Read the WHOLE story in your Bible together! You can find it in the first Gospel: Matthew 20:1-16

In the Spark Story Bible, look for "The Vineyard Workers" on pages 266.

The Greatest Commandment

The Pharisees (FAIR-ih-seez) were Jewish leaders who tried to make sure everyone was following the laws of faith. They asked Jesus a hard question to trick him: What is the greatest commandment: loving God or loving our neighbors? Jesus was not afraid of their trick. He answered that the most important rule is to love God with our hearts, souls, and minds *and* to love our neighbors. Jesus helped people know more about God's love by answering questions.

How do you learn about God? Who answers your questions?

Key Verse

Jesus replied: "'Love the Lord your God with all your heart and with all your soul and with all your mind.' This is the first and greatest commandment. And the second is like it: 'Love your neighbor as yourself.'"

Matthew 22:37-39

> **DEAR JESUS, help us to ask questions and listen for your answers. Amen.**

Try this!

Many people asked Jesus questions. Play a question game: Make a puppet with an old sock or small paper sack, or use a puppet you already have. One family member puts on the puppet, and everyone else asks the puppet a question. If the puppet can answer, that person keeps the puppet. Pass the puppet if you can't answer a question.

There's MORE to this story!

Read the WHOLE story in your Bible together! You can find it in the first book in the New Testament: Matthew 22:34-46

In the Spark Story Bible, look for "The Greatest Commandment" on page 268.

Jesus Blesses the Children

One day Jesus was speaking to a large crowd. Everyone wanted to see Jesus. Some children moved in closer. Jesus' disciples tried to shoo the kids away. "Wait!" Jesus said. "I want the children to sit by me." When they came to him, he blessed them and told the disciples that children understand God in special ways, so they should learn from them. Children are important in the kingdom of God!

When have you felt important because you are a child? When have you felt ignored?

Key Verse

When Jesus saw this, he was indignant. He said to them, "Let the little children come to me, and do not hinder them, for the kingdom of God belongs to such as these."

Mark 10:14

> **DEAR GOD, thank you for loving kids like me! Amen.**

✨🐸 Try this!

You can practice telling stories about Jesus to others. Put your dolls, stuffed animals, or action figures in a circle. Sit down and pretend to be Jesus. Open your Spark Story Bible or another children's Bible and show your "audience" stories about God.

📖 There's MORE to this story!

Read the WHOLE story in your Bible together! You can find it in the second book in the New Testament: Mark 10:13-16

In the Spark Story Bible, look for "Jesus Blesses the Children" on page 272.

A Rich Man's Questions

A rich man asked Jesus, "What should I do so God will love me forever?" Jesus replied, "Give everything away and follow me." The man was shocked! Jesus explained, "It's easier for a camel to walk through the eye of a needle than for greedy people to enter God's kingdom! Nothing we do wins us God's love. Nothing we do makes us lose God's love. God's love is a forever love."

What things would be hard to give away? What things would be easy to give away?

Key Verse

Jesus looked at him and loved him. "One thing you lack," he said. "Go, sell everything you have and give to the poor, and you will have treasure in heaven. Then come, follow me."

Mark 10:21

> LOVING GOD, help us to share your love by sharing with others the good things you have given us. Amen.

Try this!

Learn how to thread a needle and sew a button while making a fun camel puppet! Get an old brown sock, a couple of buttons for eyes, thread, and a needle. Have an adult help you sew the button eyes on the sock puppet. Give your camel puppet a name and practice telling the story of the rich man's questions with the puppet.

There's MORE to this story!

Read the WHOLE story in your Bible together! You can find it in the shortest Gospel: Mark 10:17-31

In the Spark Story Bible, look for "A Rich Man's Questions" on page 278.

Bartimaeus Sees

Jesus was leaving the town of Jericho when he passed by a blind man named Bartimaeus. Bartimaeus had faith in Jesus. He shouted, "Jesus, have mercy on me!" Bartimaeus told Jesus he wanted to see again. Jesus said, "Your faith has made you well." It was a miracle! Bartimaeus could see!

How do you ask Jesus for help? What could you ask Jesus to help you with?

Key Verse

When he heard that it was Jesus of Nazareth, he began to shout, "Jesus, Son of David, have mercy on me!"

Mark 10:47

JESUS, have mercy on me and take care of me when I need your help. Amen.

Try this!

Find two cans and a long piece of string. Ask an adult to poke a hole through the bottom of the cans, pull the string through the holes, and tie knots. Have a friend take one can across the room. Read today's story into your can while your friend listens to his or her can. Did your friend hear the message?

There's MORE to this story!

Read the WHOLE story in your Bible together! You can find it in the second Gospel: Mark 10:46-52

In the Spark Story Bible, look for "Bartimaeus Sees" on page 280.

The Widow's Offering

Jesus was teaching near the Temple moneybox where people gave offerings. "The rich people wear beautiful clothes and are treated with respect," Jesus said. "But see! Some rich people give money to show off." Jesus saw a poor widow putting two small coins in the moneybox. "She doesn't have much money," Jesus said. "But see! She quietly gives all she has."

Can you think of someone who gives quietly? When have you given a surprise gift?

Key Verse

They all gave out of their wealth; but she, out of her poverty, put in everything—all she had to live on.

Mark 12:44

> **DEAR JESUS, help us not to show off when we give. Help us to be quietly generous. Amen.**

✨ Try this!

Find a big jar and decorate it with markers, glued-on tissue paper, or pictures from magazines. Write the word "Stealth Giving" on the jar and put it somewhere everyone can reach. Every time you find some spare change, try to sneak it into the jar without anyone seeing. See how long it takes to fill up! When the jar is full, donate the money to a church or charity.

📖 There's MORE to this story!

Read the WHOLE story in your Bible together! You can find it in the second New Testament book: Mark 12:38-44

In the Spark Story Bible, look for "The Widow's Offering" on page 284.

Four Friends

Four friends had a friend who couldn't walk. They knew Jesus could help their friend, but Jesus was in a house crowded with people, and they couldn't get their friend in. The man's friends carried him to the roof and used ropes to lower him into the room. Jesus forgave the man's sins and healed him!

How can you help friends?
How do friends help you?

Key Verse

When Jesus saw their faith, he said, "Friend, your sins are forgiven."

Luke 5:20

> GOD, please be with our friends!
> Help us to be there for them
> when they need us. Amen.

Try this!

Find a friend about your size and work together to lift each other up. Sit on the ground back to back. Link your arms together and then stand up by pushing against each other. How hard is it to lift each other up? How hard would it have been for the four friends to carry the man to Jesus?

There's MORE to this story!

Read the WHOLE story in your Bible together! You can find it in the third book in the New Testament: Luke 5:17-26

In the Spark Story Bible, look for "Four Friends" on page 288.

Banquet with Simon

Jesus was eating dinner at his friend Simon's house when a woman came in. She washed Jesus' feet with her tears, dried them with her hair, and rubbed them with oil. Simon was upset. He thought the woman should not have done that because of mistakes she had made in her life. Jesus praised the woman for her act of love and forgave her sins.

When have you needed forgiveness? Who forgave you?

Key Verse

Then Jesus said to her, "Your sins are forgiven."

Luke 7:48

Try this!

Make a puzzle that shows forgiveness. Find a picture of two or more happy people from a magazine or the Internet. Glue it on a piece of heavy paper and then cut it into pieces. Mix the pieces up and try to put the puzzle back together. When we forgive or are forgiven, we are putting a relationship back together!

There's MORE to this story!

Read the WHOLE story in your Bible together! You can find it in the third Gospel: Luke 7:36-50

In the Spark Story Bible, look for "Banquet with Simon" on page 294.

The Transfiguration

Peter, James, John, and Jesus were climbing a mountain together. As they got to the top, Jesus became all bright and shiny! Then Moses and Elijah appeared. How was this possible? Moses and Elijah had been dead for many, many, MANY years. A voice boomed: "This is my Son. Listen to him." Then everything went back to normal. We call this event in Jesus' life the *Transfiguration*.

What would you have done if you saw the Transfiguration? When have you seen something amazing?

Key Verse

After six days Jesus took Peter, James and John with him and led them up a high mountain, where they were all alone. There he was transfigured before them.

Mark 9:2

> DEAR JESUS, help us to see you in the ordinary and the extraordinary. You are an amazing God! Amen.

 Try this!

Remember Jesus' "glowing" transfiguration by taking some glowing pictures of you and your family or friends. You'll need glow sticks, a camera, and an adult to use the camera. Use the glow sticks to create rings and necklaces. Go outside after dark and twirl the rings around your arms and other parts of your body while someone takes pictures. (This activity works best if you turn off the flash.)

There's MORE to this story!

Read the WHOLE story in your Bible together! You can find it in three Gospel books: Matthew 17:1-13; Mark 9:2-9; Luke 9:28-36

In the Spark Story Bible, look for "The Transfiguration" on page 298.

The Good Samaritan

Jesus told a story about a man who was attacked by robbers. He was hurt and needed help. A priest and another religious man passed and did not help. A Samaritan stopped and helped, even though everyone, including the man who was hurt, was mean to Samaritans. Jesus said the Samaritan was an example of a good neighbor—because he helped the man who needed it, whether he was a friend or not!

Who are your neighbors? How do neighbors help each other?

Key Verse

"Which of these three do you think was a neighbor to the man who fell into the hands of robbers?" The expert in the law replied, "The one who had mercy on him." Jesus told him, "Go and do likewise."

Luke 10:36-37

> ## JESUS, you hold us together in love. Help us to share your love with everyone around us. Amen.

Try this!

The injured man in this story was traveling from Jerusalem to Jericho. Go online with a parent and enter "Jerusalem to Jericho distance" in a search engine. How far are the cities from each other? How long would it take to walk that distance?

📖 There's MORE to this story!

Read the WHOLE story in your Bible together! You can find it in the Gospel of Luke. Gospel stories like this are called parables: Luke 10:25-37

In the Spark Story Bible, look for "The Good Samaritan" on page 300.

Mary and Martha

Jesus visited sisters Martha and Mary. Mary listened to Jesus teach. Martha cooked and cleaned and prepared food for them. She thought she was doing all the work. Martha got mad at Mary. Jesus said it was good that Mary was making time to listen and learn from him.

What keeps you busy? When do you make time for Jesus?

Key Verse

"Martha, Martha," the Lord answered, "you are worried and upset about many things, but few things are needed—or indeed only one. Mary has chosen what is better, and it will not be taken away from her."

Luke 10:41-42

> **DEAR JESUS, we are so busy with activities. Help us to find time for you every day. Amen.**

⭐🐸 Try this!

Gather around your family calendar. Remember fun things you did in the past week. Add new activities for next week. Make decisions together about making time for Jesus during your week. Then say this blessing over your family calendar: Dear God, bless our activities. Bless our time. Bless our family. Amen.

📖 There's MORE to this story!

Read the WHOLE story in your Bible together! You can find it in the book between Mark and John: Luke 10:38-42

In the Spark Story Bible, look for "Mary and Martha" on page 306.

The Lost Sheep and Lost Coin

Jesus told these stories: A shepherd had 100 sheep and loved them all. One day, he counted only 99. One was lost! The shepherd searched and searched until he found his lost sheep. The shepherd rejoiced! A woman saved ten coins. One day, she counted only nine. One was lost! She looked and looked until she found the coin. The woman rejoiced! And God rejoices when what was lost is found!

When have you lost something? How long did you search for it?

Key Verse

In the same way, I tell you, there is rejoicing in the presence of the angels of God over one sinner who repents.

Luke 15:10

DEAR JESUS, thank you for always finding us. Thank you for staying close to us. Amen.

Try this!

Play a sheep hide-and-seek game. One person hides a stuffed sheep or another stuffed animal somewhere in your home. Everyone else searches for the sheep, asking up to ten "yes" or "no" questions. How many questions does it take to find the missing sheep? The person who finds the sheep may celebrate like the shepherd and then hide the sheep for the next round.

There's MORE to this story!

Read the WHOLE story in your Bible together! You can find it in the third New Testament book: Luke 15:1-10

In the Spark Story Bible, look for "The Lost Sheep and Lost Coin" on page 312.

The Prodigal Son

Jesus told this story. A son took money from his father, left home, and wasted it all on parties and food. He became hungry, lonely, and sad. His older brother stayed home and worked. The younger brother came home, begging to at least be taken in as a servant. Instead, his father welcomed him joyfully and threw him a party. The older brother was upset. But the father said, "You have always been with me! But your brother left, and now he is home!" God welcomes us so we can welcome others, just like this father.

How do you welcome people? Who welcomes you?

Key Verse

"My son," the father said, "you are always with me, and everything I have is yours. But we had to celebrate and be glad, because this brother of yours was dead and is alive again; he was lost and is found."

Luke 15:31-32

JESUS, you always welcome us home. Help us to welcome everyone. Amen.

✨ Try this!

Many cultures welcome people with dance. As a family, watch a video of a welcome dance from Liberia. Search for "Liberian Welcome Dance Video." Make up your own family welcome dance. Do the dance the next time a family member comes home.

📖 There's MORE to this story!

Read the WHOLE story in your Bible together! You can find it in the third book of the New Testament: Luke 15:11-31

In the Spark Story Bible, look for "The Prodigal Son" on page 316.

Ten Men Healed

Ten men who were sick called out to Jesus. "Jesus, have mercy on us!" they cried. Jesus told the men to go see the priests. The men went to the Temple, and as they walked, they became well! One man went back and thanked Jesus. "Where are the other nine men?" Jesus asked. "Don't they want to praise God?" Then Jesus told the man, "Get up and go. Your faith heals you."

When do you say "thank you"? Have you ever forgotten to say it?

Key Verse

One of them, when he saw he was healed, came back, praising God in a loud voice. He threw himself at Jesus' feet and thanked him—and he was a Samaritan.

Luke 17:15-16

> GOD, we are thankful for all the good things you give us every day. Amen.

 Try this!

Have fun making thank-you cards. Gather card stock and markers. Fold the card stock into cards. Draw pictures of today's story and other things that show how you praise God. Write "THANK YOU" inside the cards. Save the cards for times when you need to thank someone.

There's MORE to this story!

Read the WHOLE story in your Bible together! You can find it in the third New Testament book: Luke 17:11-19

In the Spark Story Bible, look for "Ten Men Healed" on page 322.

157

Zacchaeus

Zacchaeus was a tax collector who lived in Jericho. People hated Zacchaeus because he took their money. Jesus went to Zacchaeus's house for dinner and told him that God wants us to love each other. Zacchaeus listened, changed his ways, and returned the money he had taken.

Why do we sometimes hate others? How can we love instead?

Key Verse

When Jesus reached the spot, he looked up and said to him, "Zacchaeus, come down immediately. I must stay at your house today." So he came down at once and welcomed him gladly.

Luke 19:5-6

> **DEAR JESUS, sometimes we make bad choices. We know that you can help us change, like you helped Zacchaeus. Amen.**

Try this!

Zacchaeus climbed a tree to see Jesus. Climbing trees is fun, but finding a good climbing tree can be hard. Go on a family walk. Look for big trees with low branches. The branches you climb must be as big as the top of your arm. Have an adult help you climb and keep you safe. What do you see?

There's MORE to this story!

Read the WHOLE story in your Bible together! You can find it near the end of the third Gospel, the book of Luke: Luke 19:1-10

In the Spark Story Bible, look for "Zacchaeus" on page 326.

Wedding at Cana

Jesus was with his friends at a wedding party. Suddenly the wine ran out! Jesus' mother, Mary, asked Jesus to help. Jesus took six large clay jars of water and turned the water into wine. The party could go on! This was Jesus' first miracle, and everyone was amazed. Jesus' friends knew he was God's Son.

What things do you celebrate?
How do you celebrate?

Key Verse

What Jesus did here in Cana of Galilee was the first of the signs through which he revealed his glory; and his disciples believed in him.

John 2:11

GOD, thank you for all the wonderful things we have to celebrate together! Amen.

 Try this!

We can celebrate Jesus anytime. Invite friends over for a party like the one in this story. Serve grape juice and tell your friends the story of Jesus' miracle. Then dance to music and praise God!

📖 **There's MORE to this story!**

Read the WHOLE story in your Bible together! You can find it in the fourth book in the New Testament: John 2:1-11

In the Spark Story Bible, look for "Wedding at Cana" on page 332.

Woman at the Well

After a long walk in a place called Samaria, Jesus stopped to rest at a well. A Samaritan woman saw him and gave him a drink of water from the well. Jesus offered her a different kind of water. He called it "living water." The woman realized that Jesus was the Messiah, the Savior, and ran to tell everyone.

What's your favorite drink when you are thirsty? Why?

Key Verse

Jesus answered, "Everyone who drinks this water will be thirsty again, but whoever drinks the water I give them will never thirst. Indeed, the water I give them will become in them a spring of water welling up to eternal life."

John 4:13-14

> **DEAR JESUS, thank you for filling us up with your living water of love, forgiveness, and new life. Amen.**

Try this!

Samaritans were outcasts in Jesus' time. Many Jewish people didn't want to be near them. Jesus reached out to the Samaritan woman anyway. How can your family show kindness to someone who might feel left out in your community? Can you visit an elderly person? Volunteer to serve at a soup kitchen? Smile at everyone you see today?

There's MORE to this story!

Read the WHOLE story in your Bible together! You can find it in the New Testament, in the fourth Gospel: John 4:5-42

In the Spark Story Bible, look for "Woman at the Well" on page 338.

Jesus Feeds 5,000

A crowd came to hear Jesus. Jesus and the disciples knew the men, women, and children were hungry. What would Jesus do? A boy offered his lunch to Jesus: two fish and five loaves of bread. Jesus blessed and shared the food with 5,000 people, and it was enough to feed them all. It was a miracle!

What is it like to be hungry?
What have you shared?

Key Verse

Jesus then took the loaves, gave thanks, and distributed to those who were seated as much as they wanted. He did the same with the fish.

John 6:11

DEAR JESUS, thanks for feeding us. Help us to share what we have. Amen.

 Try this!

There are people in our communities without enough food to eat. Find a local nonprofit that serves meals or provides food for people in your community and find out how you can volunteer. Invite a friend to join you and your family! Before you go, pray for the people and ask God to bless them.

There's MORE to this story!

Read the WHOLE story in your Bible together! You can find it in the fourth Gospel book: John 6:1-14

In the Spark Story Bible, look for "Jesus Feeds 5,000" on page 344.

The Good Shepherd

Jesus called himself the "good shepherd" and told people that they were his sheep. To help people understand, Jesus told a story about a little lamb who was lost and the loving shepherd who searched for the lamb and kept it safe. Jesus said that he loves and cares for every sheep in his flock, just like a good shepherd.

> How do you feel when you lose something? How do you feel when it's found?

Key Verse

"I am the good shepherd; I know my sheep and my sheep know me—just as the Father knows me and I know the Father—and I lay down my life for the sheep."

John 10:14

> **DEAR JESUS, you are my shepherd. Find me when I am lost and care for me forever. Amen.**

 Try this!

Play a game of shepherd hide-and-seek with your family, with one person as the shepherd who has to find the sheep in the flock, and one "wolf" who wants to find them first! Everyone else is the sheep. Take turns being the shepherd, sheep, and wolf. What is it like to be found by the shepherd? What is it like to be found by the wolf? What is it like to be the shepherd, responsible for the safety of the sheep?

There's MORE to this story!

Read the WHOLE story in your Bible together! You can find it in the last Gospel: John 10:11-18

In the Spark Story Bible, look for "The Good Shepherd" on page 350.

Lazarus

Mary, Martha, and Lazarus were Jesus' friends. When Lazarus died, Jesus cried. He went to the tomb and said, "Lazarus, come out!" Lazarus did come out! The people were amazed. Jesus brought Lazarus back to life.

> Why do people cry? When was the last time you cried?

Key Verse

Jesus said to her, "I am the resurrection and the life. The one who believes in me will live, even though they die; and whoever lives by believing in me will never die. Do you believe this?"

John 11:25-26

DEAR LORD, thank you for hands to help my friends, to hug them, and to celebrate with them when they have a good day. I always want to use my hands to serve you and love others. Amen.

⭐ Try this!

Families need everyone's hands to help. Trace all the hands in your family on paper. Cut out your hands and write your names on them. Set a timer for five minutes. Look for different places in your home where you can help. Tape one hand near each place. When the timer rings, tell each other how you will help.

📖 There's MORE to this story!

Read the WHOLE story in your Bible together! You can find it in the fourth Gospel, the fourth book of the New Testament: John 11:1-45

In the Spark Story Bible, look for "Lazarus" on page 354.

Palm Sunday

Jesus rode into Jerusalem on a donkey. His friends, the disciples, followed him while people made a special path of palm branches for Jesus. They shouted, "Hosanna! God's King!" This made the priests angry. They didn't like that the crowd was calling Jesus king.

When do you cheer? What cheer would you shout to Jesus?

Key Verse

Hosanna to the Son of David! Blessed is he who comes in the name of the Lord! Hosanna in the highest heaven!

Matthew 21:9

DEAR GOD, Jesus followed a path to Jerusalem. Help me follow your ways every day to get closer to you. Amen.

Try this!

On the first Palm Sunday, date palms were used. These palms have trunks one foot (30 cm) in diameter and grow slowly. Dates are the fruit of these trees. Go to a local plant store, nursery, or garden to see palms growing. Bring a tape measure and figure out how big or small they are. Try growing a palm or eating a date at home and think of Jesus when you do.

There's MORE to this story!

Read the WHOLE story in your Bible together! You can find it in three different Gospels. Read all three versions: Matthew 21:1-11; Mark 11:1-11; Luke 19:28-40

In the Spark Story Bible, look for "Palm Sunday" on page 358.

The Last Supper

Jesus ate supper with his 12 best friends, the disciples. He washed their feet. He blessed bread and shared it. He gave thanks and shared wine. Jesus knew that he would not be with them much longer. He wanted to show the disciples his love and enjoy his last meal with them.

What foods do you share?
Why do people eat together?

Key Verse

Now that I, your Lord and Teacher, have washed your feet, you also should wash one another's feet.

John 13:14

JESUS, we are all at your table.
Help us love one another. Amen.

Try this!

Jesus showed love to his disciples by washing their feet. Follow Jesus' example with your family! Fill a basin with warm water, grab a towel, and take turns washing each other's feet. Tell each other what you love about each other during the foot washing.

There's MORE to this story!

Read the WHOLE story in your Bible together! You can find it in all four Gospels: Matthew 26:17-30; Mark 14:10-32; Luke 22:14-28; John 13:1-20

In the Spark Story Bible, look for "The Last Supper" on page 364.

Jesus Is Betrayed

Jesus was facing hard times. Instead of helping him, Jesus' friends—his disciples—let him down. Jesus asked his friends to pray with him, but they fell asleep. One disciple named Judas told Jesus' enemies where to find him. Another disciple, Peter, pretended he didn't know Jesus. But Jesus never gave up on his friends.

Has a friend ever disappointed you? What do you do when you're sorry?

Key Verse

Then Peter remembered the word Jesus had spoken: "Before the rooster crows, you will disown me three times." And he went outside and wept bitterly.

Matthew 26:75

> **DEAR GOD, when we are weak, you make us strong. We'll follow you all our lives long! Amen.**

Try this!

Make rock candy in honor of Peter; his nickname was the Rock! With an adult, heat two cups of sugar and one cup of water in a saucepan. Add food coloring and two more cups of sugar. Stir until the mixture dissolves. Don't let it boil! Pour it into clean jar. Tie a 6-inch piece of string to a craft stick and lay the stick across the jar's top (so the string hangs into the mixture). The rock candy will form over several days. Retell the story of Jesus and Peter when you enjoy your candy.

There's MORE to this story!

Read the WHOLE story in your Bible together! You can find it in three Gospels in the New Testament: Matthew 26:31-75; Mark 14:26-72; Luke 22:32-71

In the Spark Story Bible, look for "Jesus Is Betrayed" on page 370.

The Day Jesus Died

Soldiers arrested Jesus and pushed a crown of thorns onto his head. They made him carry a heavy wooden cross through the streets. Crowds gathered and yelled at Jesus. The soldiers nailed him to the cross. Jesus prayed and asked God to forgive them all. Finally, he died. It was a sad day.

> Why did Jesus love those who hurt him? When have you forgiven someone?

Key Verse

Jesus said, "Father, forgive them, for they do not know what they are doing."

Luke 23:34a

> **Dear Jesus, thank you for dying for me! Thank you for loving me! Amen.**

✨ Try this!

Even before we were born, Jesus loved us so much that he was willing to die for us. He is our truest friend. Make a bracelet as a reminder that Jesus loves you: Take six long pieces of colored embroidery floss and braid them together. Measure the finished piece to fit your wrist. Tie it, cut off any extra floss, and wear it. Make a second bracelet and give it to a friend.

📖 There's MORE to this story!

Read the WHOLE story in your Bible together! You can find it in the first three books of the New Testament: Matthew 27:27-66; Mark 15:21-47; Luke 23:26-56

In the Spark Story Bible, look for "The Day Jesus Died" on page 376.

The Empty Tomb

Jesus' body was put in a tomb. On the third day after Jesus died, women came to take care of the body. The tomb was open! The stone was rolled away! The body was gone! An angel told them, "Jesus is alive!" The women had a job to do. They went to tell everyone the good news!

What good news do you share? Who hears your good news?

Key Verse

In their fright the women bowed down with their faces to the ground, but the men said to them, "Why do you look for the living among the dead? He is not here; he has risen!"

Luke 24:5-6a

> **Jesus is alive today and every day! The rock was rolled away. Thanks be to God! Amen.**

 Try this!

The women who visited Jesus' tomb couldn't wait to tell the good news. Remember them while playing this "hurry up" game. Go outside and form two teams for a relay race. Take turns racing to a certain point and back while carrying an egg on a spoon. The first team to have all its members finish the relay— without breaking an egg—wins!

There's MORE to this story!

Read the WHOLE story in your Bible together! You can find it in three Gospels: Matthew 28:1-10; Mark 16:1-8; Luke 24:1-12

In the Spark Story Bible, look for "The Empty Tomb" on page 382

The Road to Emmaus

Three days after Jesus died, a man named Cleopas and his friend were walking to the town of Emmaus. They were very sad about what had happened to Jesus, and while they walked, they talked about it. Suddenly, another man began walking with them. The man explained to them why Jesus had to die and told them everything would be all right because Jesus really was the Son of God. The friends started to feel better. They invited the new man to eat supper with them. Later at dinner, the man blessed bread and offered it to the friends. Suddenly, the friends recognized who the man was—it was Jesus! Jesus was really alive!

Have you ever not recognized a friend? Who always recognizes you?

Key Verse

When he was at the table with them, he took bread,
gave thanks, broke it and began to give it to them.
Then their eyes were opened and they recognized him,
and he disappeared from their sight.

Luke 24:30-31

> JESUS, you really are alive! Help us see
> you in the world and in our lives. Amen.

 Try this!

Make *cascarones*, or confetti eggs. Crack an egg at the
top, opening a small hole and pour out the yoke. Dry
the eggshell. Fill with confetti, and glue a piece of tissue
paper over the open end. Decorate the outside in festive
colors. Crack the eggs in celebration and as a reminder
that they are empty, like Jesus' tomb. Jesus is alive!

There's MORE to this story!

Read the WHOLE story in your Bible together! You can find
it in the third book in the New Testament: Luke 24:13-35

In the Spark Story Bible, look for "The Road to Emmaus" on page 388.

Doubting Thomas

The disciples were sad and scared when Jesus died. But a few days later, Jesus appeared to them and told them that he would always be in their hearts! Thomas wasn't with the group, but when he arrived, the excited disciples told him that Jesus was alive and had appeared to them. "I'll believe when I see," he said. Later, Jesus appeared again to the disciples while Thomas was there. Jesus invited Thomas to touch the wounds in his hands and side. It was really him! "Don't doubt anymore," Jesus told Thomas. "My Lord and my God!" Thomas exclaimed.

What one thing do you wonder about Jesus?
Who could you ask a question about Jesus?

Key Verse

Then [Jesus] said to Thomas, "Put your finger here; see my hands. Reach out your hand and put it into my side. Stop doubting and believe."

John 20:27

GOD, when we have questions or doubts, help us to trust in you. Thank you for loving us! Amen.

Try this!

Thomas was called "the Twin" (John 20:24). Jesus gave Peter the nickname "the Rock" (John 1:42). What nickname might Jesus pick for you? Think of loving nicknames for each person in your family. Print a family photo or draw a picture of your family, and label each person with his or her nickname.

There's MORE to this story!

Read the WHOLE story in your Bible together! You can find it in the fourth Gospel: John 20:19-31

In the Spark Story Bible, look for "Doubting Thomas" on page 392.

The Great Commission

After rising from the dead, Jesus visited his disciples. They were excited to see him again! "Go everywhere in the world," Jesus said. "Baptize people, and teach them about me. And remember, I will always be with you." Then Jesus went to heaven, and the disciples went to work!

Who first told you about Jesus? What's your favorite story about Jesus?

Key Verse

Therefore go and make disciples of all nations, baptizing them in the name of the Father and of the Son and of the Holy Spirit.

Matthew 28:19

DEAR GOD, give us the words to go into the world and tell everyone about Jesus! Amen.

 Try this!

Missionaries go all over the world to tell people about Jesus. Do you know any missionaries? If not, ask if any missionaries are being supported by your church. Find out the name and address of a missionary and write that person a letter. What does the missionary do? How can you help?

There's MORE to this story!

Read the WHOLE story in your Bible together! You can find it in three books: Matthew 28:16-20; Luke 24:36-53; Acts 1:6-14

In the Spark Story Bible, look for "The Great Commission" on page 396.

The Ascension

After Jesus died and rose again, he gave his disciples important instructions. "God is doing amazing things, and your help is needed!" he said. "Tell your friends, families, and everyone you meet about me!" Then Jesus rose into the air. "What's happening?" the disciples wondered. Two men in white robes appeared. "Don't worry!" they said. "Jesus will return someday."

Who can you tell about Jesus?
What would you say?

Key Verse

"Men of Galilee," they said, "why do you stand here looking into the sky? This same Jesus, who has been taken from you into heaven, will come back in the same way you have seen him go into heaven."

Acts 1:11

DEAR JESUS, help us to keep telling your story until you come again. Amen.

 Try this!

Enjoy storytelling time with your family. Cuddle together. Give each person a chance to share what they think is the most important thing people should know about Jesus and why. Practice telling those things to each other and then think of someone outside your family you can tell later.

There's MORE to this story!

Read the WHOLE story in your Bible together! You can find it in two New Testament books: Luke 24:50-53; Acts 1:6-14

In the Spark Story Bible, look for "The Ascension" on page 398.

The Holy Spirit

Jesus' disciples were celebrating the festival of Pentecost. WHOOSH! A strong wind blew. Fiery flames appeared above each disciple's head. The disciples even started speaking in different languages! This was the Holy Spirit—just like Jesus promised! With the help of God's Spirit, the disciples started living new lives and boldly telling everyone about Jesus.

Who are helpers in your life? How do they help you?

Key Verse

All of them were filled with the Holy Spirit and began to speak in other tongues as the Spirit enabled them.

Acts 2:4

HOLY SPIRIT, we can't see you, but like the wind, we know you are here. Help us know your power and peace. Amen.

 Try this!

Make a Pentecost pinwheel to remind you of the Holy Spirit! With an adult's help, find a free, printable pinwheel pattern and directions on the Internet. Use red paper to represent the fire that appeared on the disciples' heads. You'll also need scissors, a hole punch, a straw, and brass fasteners. Make two and share one with friend, telling your friend about God's Spirit who moves our hearts, like wind moves a pinwheel!

There's MORE to this story!

Read the WHOLE story in your Bible together! You can find it in the fifth book in the New Testament: Acts 2:1-21, 36-42

In the Spark Story Bible, look for "The Holy Spirit" on page 400.

Early Believers

Early believers in Jesus shared everything: food, clothes, money, and even their homes. There was enough for everyone. They met together to talk about Jesus and thank God. When other people saw how happy the believers were, they became Christians too. The church family grew and grew.

What do you share? How does sharing make you feel?

Key Verse

They devoted themselves to the apostles' teaching and to fellowship, to the breaking of bread and to prayer.

Acts 2:42

> DEAR GOD, help us to share with others so that your family keeps growing and growing. Amen.

 Try this!

When Christians get together today, they do some of the same things the early believers did 2,000 years ago: pray, worship, eat together, talk about Jesus, and help others. However, early Christians met in homes, not church buildings! Invite some friends and family over and have a worship service at home! Sing songs, read a Bible story, and pray together—just like the early believers!

There's MORE to this story!

Read the WHOLE story in your Bible together! You can find it in the first book after the Gospels: Acts 2:42-47; 4:32-37

In the Spark Story Bible, look for "Early Believers" on page 402.

Peter Heals

Peter and John were walking to the Temple when they met a man who could not walk at the gate. Because he couldn't walk, he couldn't work, so he begged for money to buy food. He asked Peter and John, "Would you please give me some money for food?" Peter said, "We don't have any money, but I have something better. In Jesus' name, I say, get up and walk!" The man leapt up and began to walk, then dance, skip and hop as he praised God.

How can you help people without giving money? What do you have that you can share?

Key Verse

Then Peter said, "Silver or gold I do not have, but what I do have I give you. In the name of Jesus Christ of Nazareth, walk."

Acts 3:6

DEAR GOD, thank you for healing people! Thank you for helping me help others! Amen.

 Try this!

Are there people in your community who are homeless or need to beg for money? There are many ways you can show them love that don't involve money! Brainstorm some ideas as a family and then volunteer with a local nonprofit that does outreach to people experiencing poverty in your community.

There's MORE to this story!

Read the WHOLE story in your Bible together! You can find it in the fifth book in the New Testament: Acts 3:1-16

In the Spark Story Bible, look for "Peter Heals" on page 404.

Saul to Paul

A man named Saul hated Jesus. A man named Ananias loved Jesus. God had plans for both men! God blinded Saul with a bright light. Then God told Ananias to find Saul and pray for him. When Ananias prayed, Saul was filled with the Holy Spirit, and he could see again. Saul became known as Paul, and he spent the rest of his life teaching others how to follow Jesus.

What are your plans? What do you think God's plans are for you?

Key Verse

At once he began to preach in the synagogues that Jesus is the Son of God.

Acts 9:20

> # GOD, help us to make plans this week and remember you in our plans. Amen.

☄ Try this!

Paul traveled to the city of Damascus, located in modern-day Syria. A popular snack in that area of the world is Syrian bread topped with honey and sesame seeds. To make a version of this at home, lightly toast a piece of pita bread. Spread butter, honey, and sesame seeds inside the pocket. Enjoy while the bread is warm.

📖 There's MORE to this story!

Read the WHOLE story in your Bible together! You can find it in the book that follows the Gospels: Acts 9:1-20

In the Spark Story Bible, look for "Saul to Paul" on page 408.

An Angel Frees Peter

Peter was put in prison because King Herod didn't like the good news he shared about God. One night, an angel woke Peter up. "Get up quickly and follow me!" the angel said, and he led Peter right out of the prison! Peter went to a friend's house to show that he was free. A girl named Rhoda heard Peter at the gate. She was so excited to tell everyone the good news that she forgot to let Peter in the door! Oops!

Key Verse

When she recognized Peter's voice, she was so overjoyed she ran back without opening it and exclaimed, "Peter is at the door!"

Acts 12:14

GOD, help me to take risks like Peter did to share your good news! Please be with me. Amen.

Try this!

What is your good news? Share stories with your family about good news that you heard about or that happened to you by writing pretend newspaper articles or creating colorful posters. See who can share their good news with the most excitement!

There's MORE to this story!

Read the WHOLE story in your Bible together! You can find it in the first book after the Gospels: Acts 12:1-19

In the Spark Story Bible, look for "An Angel Frees Peter" on page 414.

Lydia

Paul traveled to many places to teach people about Jesus. In one faraway city, he met a woman named Lydia. Lydia made purple cloth and sold it to people for clothes. She wanted to learn all about Jesus! Paul baptized Lydia and everyone in her family. Lydia invited Paul to her home and shared her love, faith, and money with others.

Who do you invite into your home? How can you show hospitality?

Key Verse

One of those listening was a woman from the city of Thyatira named Lydia, a dealer in purple cloth. She was a worshiper of God. The Lord opened her heart to respond to Paul's message.

Acts 16:14

> **DEAR JESUS, help us share your love with everyone we meet today! Amen.**

 Try this!

Have some tie-dye fun as a family! Prepare a purple dye bath, following the instructions on the fabric dye packaging. Twist a white shirt or socks and place rubber bands tightly around them for a tie-dye effect. Dunk the shirt or socks into the dye. Soak for five minutes. Place the dyed clothing in a plastic bag and let sit overnight. Wash in cold water. Think of Lydia when you wear your purple clothes!

There's MORE to this story!

Read the WHOLE story in your Bible together! You can find it in the New Testament: Acts 16:9-15

In the Spark Story Bible, look for "Lydia" on page 418.

Paul and Silas

Paul and Silas liked to tell people about God. Some leaders didn't like what they had to say and threw Paul and Silas in jail! Paul and Silas weren't afraid. They knew God was with them. An earthquake broke the jail door and their chains, but Paul and Silas didn't try to escape. They knew God still had people in the prison who needed to hear the good news about Jesus. The guard was so amazed that he believed their message about Jesus too.

When have you been amazed? What helps you believe in Jesus?

Key Verse

Believe in the Lord Jesus, and you will be saved—you and your household.

Acts 16:31

Try this!

Paul and Silas prayed and sang while they were in prison. Sometimes people sing when they are afraid to help them feel better. With an adult, search the Internet for the hymn "Swing Low, Sweet Chariot." Learn the words and tune of this song. The next time you are scared, sing like Paul and Silas to help remind you that God is with you.

There's MORE to this story!

Read the WHOLE story in your Bible together! You can find it in the fifth book in the New Testament: Acts 16:16-40

In the Spark Story Bible, look for "Paul and Silas" on page 422.

Paul's Letters

Paul loved to share the story of Jesus. Sometimes he visited people. Sometimes he wrote letters. Paul had a special message for his friends in Rome. He wrote, "God's love is amazing! Jesus came so that everyone would know how much God loves us all. Believing in Jesus changes your life."

Key Verse

To all in Rome who are loved by God and called to be his holy people: Grace and peace to you from God our Father and from the Lord Jesus Christ.

Romans 1:7

GOD, help me to share the good news that you love EVERYONE. Amen.

✨🐢 Try this!

Paul wrote 13 letters in the New Testament, but they were much longer than the letters we usually write to our friends today. The first letter was written to his friends in Rome. This letter, or book, in the Bible is called "Romans." Use your Bible to discover the other groups and individuals who received letters from Paul. HINT: Look at the 12 books after Romans. The friends who received letters from Paul are the names of those 12 books.

📖 There's MORE to this story!

Read the WHOLE story in your Bible together! You can find it in the sixth book of the New Testament: Romans 1:1-17

In the Spark Story Bible, look for "Paul's Letters" on page 426.

Many Members, One Body

Paul wrote his friends a letter to tell them that they were all important to God, even though they did different work. Paul said that God made our bodies with lots of different parts: eyes to see, ears to hear, and noses to smell. Just like each body part has its own important job, each person has special, different, important jobs to do for God.

Key Verse

Now you are the body of Christ, and each one of you is a part of it.

1 Corinthians 12:27

GOD, help us to work together with others to do your will. Amen.

 Try this!

God made our bodies to do amazing things! Your brain has billions of nerve cells that send and receive information around your whole body. Your heart beats about 100,000 times a day! Your nose can remember 50,000 different smells. Your tongue is the strongest muscle in your body. And every thumbprint is unique. Have everyone in your family add his or her thumbprint to a piece of paper. Write the Key Verse on it and hang it somewhere to remind you to work together as one body.

There's MORE to this story!

Read the WHOLE story in your Bible together! You can find it in Paul's first letter to the Corinthians: 1 Corinthians 12:12-31

In the Spark Story Bible, look for "Many Members, One Body" on page 428.

Love Is . . .

Paul's friends in Corinth had forgotten how important love is. Paul wrote them a letter reminding them what real love looks like. Real love is patient, kind, forgiving, trusting, and hopeful. Love is not envious, boastful, rude, or selfish. Paul told his friends to remember three important things: faith, hope, and love. "The most important thing is love," Paul wrote.

How do you show love to your family? How do you show love to your friends?

Key Verse

And now these three remain: faith, hope and love. But the greatest of these is love.

1 Corinthians 13:13

> **DEAR GOD, you are the greatest! Your love is the greatest! Help us to love each other. Amen.**

 Try this!

There are lots of songs about love. But there are not many songs about the kind of love Paul writes about! Make up a song to a well-known tune about the kind of love Paul describes in 1 Corinthians 13:4-7. Add some actions too. Sing your song for family and friends and teach it to them too!

There's MORE to this story!

Read the WHOLE story in your Bible together! You can find it in the first letter Paul wrote to friends at Corinth: 1 Corinthians 13

In the Spark Story Bible, look for "Love Is . . ." on page 432.

Fruit of the Spirit

The people in a church in the city of Galatia were always arguing! Grumble. Grrrr. Arggh! Paul wrote them a letter explaining how God wanted them to live. He said they should grow "fruit" of the Spirit. He didn't mean to grow apples, pears, or bananas. Paul meant to practice things like love, kindness, patience, gentleness, and generosity. The Galatians learned about God's love and started showing it to each other.

> What fruit of the Spirit do you see in your life? What fruit do you want to see more of?

Key Verse

The fruit of the Spirit is love, joy, peace, forbearance, kindness, goodness, faithfulness, gentleness and self-control. Against such things there is no law.

Galatians 5:22-23

> **GOD, help us to grow to live in love and peace. Amen.**

Try this!

With an adult, search the Internet for a fruit pizza recipe. This kind of "pizza" usually involves a cookie-type crust and cream cheese mixture topped with different kinds of fruit. Have everyone in your family choose a favorite fruit to add to the pizza. While you work together, practice kindness, joy, gentleness, love, and patience with one another. When you are done, practice generosity—another fruit of the Spirit—by sharing the pizza with neighbors or friends. Tell your guests about the fruit of the Spirit while you enjoy your creation.

There's MORE to this story!

Read the WHOLE story in your Bible together! You can find it in the book written to people in the city of Galatia: Galatians 5:16-26

In the Spark Story Bible, look for "Fruit of the Spirit" on page 436.

Paul and the Philippians

Paul told many people about Jesus. Some people didn't like what he said, so they put him in jail. That didn't stop Paul! From jail, Paul wrote to Christian friends in Philippi. "God is with me even in jail," Paul wrote. "God will always be with you too."

Do you like to write? What can you write about Jesus?

Key Verse

I thank my God every time I remember you.

Philippians 1:3

GOD, you are with us everywhere we go. Keep us safe and help us share your love. Amen.

Paul wrote to the Philippians from prison. Another famous man who wrote a letter from jail was Martin Luther King Jr. Check out a book about Dr. King from your library, or go online with an adult and search for information about him. Look for his letter called "Letter from Birmingham Jail." This letter was also about God's love! Tell a friend about Paul and Dr. King, using your favorite way to send a message.

There's MORE to this story!

Read the WHOLE story in your Bible together! You can find it in the letter Paul wrote to Christians in the city of Philippi: Philippians 1:1-14

In the Spark Story Bible, look for "Paul and the Philippians" on page 440.

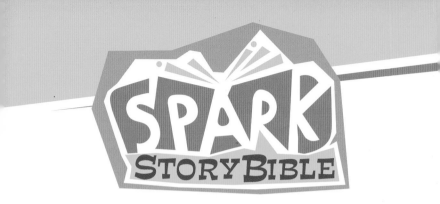

The Spark Story Bible collection sparks faith in the lives of young children and families. Using kid-friendly language, colorful artwork, and vivid storytelling, these books take readers on a lively journey through God's Word.

Find out more at sparkhouse.org!